# TECHNOLOGY AND ECONOMIC METHODS

## RESEARCH MARKETING CHANGES

JOHN LOK

Copyright © John Lok
All Rights Reserved.

This book has been published with all efforts taken to make the material error-free after the consent of the author. However, the author and the publisher do not assume and hereby disclaim any liability to any party for any loss, damage, or disruption caused by errors or omissions, whether such errors or omissions result from negligence, accident, or any other cause.

While every effort has been made to avoid any mistake or omission, this publication is being sold on the condition and understanding that neither the author nor the publishers or printers would be liable in any manner to any person by reason of any mistake or omission in this publication or for any action taken or omitted to be taken or advice rendered or accepted on the basis of this work. For any defect in printing or binding the publishers will be liable only to replace the defective copy by another copy of this work then available.

# Contents

# Preface

Introduction
Can (AI) learning machine replace human marketing research method, e.g. survey or human psychological and micro and macro economic methods to predict consumer behaviors more accurate?

Nowadays, many businessmen or marketing research professional hope to apply different methods to predict consumer behaviors in order to know what will be future market activities and market changes to help them to choose to implement what kinds of marketing strategies more accurately.

The methods include economic environmental change prediction method, consumer individual psychological change prediction method, micro or macro behavioral economic environmental change prediction method, marketing environmental change prediction method etc. different kinds of methods which can be applied to predict how consumer behavioral changes to influence whose behavioral consumption to the manufacturer products sale within one to two years short term or three to five years middle term, even above five years long term business plans.

Whether can businessmen apply micro and macro-economic methods to assist them to analyze how marketing will change, what marketing trend will develop next month or next half year, even more than one year marketing development trend in possible?

This book has two parts. The first part indicates human analysis methods can be attempted to apply to predict when, how and why consumer behavioral changing for every kind of different business. The second part indicates whether artificial intelligence can be attempted to apply to predict when, how and why consumer behavioral chaning for every kind of different business.

In my this book first part, I shall considerate on businessmen and customers both beneficial view point to explain how to apply behavioral economic concept to predict how their specific industries marketing development trend or consumer behavioral changing trend in these micro economic (individual consumer psychological shopping change trend) and macro-economic (global every specific industry marketing changing trend) environment.

I shall indicate some specific cases industry to attempt to explain whether it has really relationship between macro and micro economic environment change factors to influence marketing development change trend as well as whether businessmen can apply micro and macro-economic methods to predict future marketing development change trend in these specific industries.

In my this book second part, I concentrate on indicate whether any artificial intelligence (AI) tools will be one kind of good consumer behavioral prediction method to be choose to apply to predict consumer behaviors. I shall indicate some examples, cases to give reasonable evidences to analyze whether (AI) tools will be one kind suitable tool to be applied to predict when and how consumer behavioral changes. If (AI) can be one kind tool to attempt to be applied to predict when and how consumer behavioral changes. Will it replace other kinds of methods to predict consumer behaviors? Does it have weaknesses to be applied to predict consumer behaviors, instead of strengths? Can it be applied to predict consumer behaviors depending on any situations of only some situation? Finally, I believe that any readers can find answers to answer above these questions in this book.

In my analysis, I conclude marketing development or marketing change trend will be influenced by consumer behavioral change model or attitude factor. Finally, I hope my readers can give opinions to make judgement to evaluate my opinions whether is right or wrong in this research topic.

# Prologue

# CHAPTER ONE

# Micro and macro-economic analysis methods solve Starbucks coffee shop faces marketing change challenges

This Starbucks case indicates how Starbucks coffee drinking business applies micro and macro-economic analysis methods to predict consumer behavior. Today, Starbucks has become world famous and brings high quality coffee and beverages to its clients over the world daily. Their well-known mission statements is: to inspire and nurture the human spirit, one person, one cup and one neighborhood at a time.

How does it apply macro and micro economic analysis methods to predict consumers' coffee taste more accurate? According to the following statistics, coffee market is large market potential in the world for this particular coffee service and production. Starbucks along with many competitors, such as Costa coffee and Mc-cafe have seized this opportunity and continue to indicate within this coffee market. It is no doubt that this coffee market can be profitable in 2012 year, the CEO of Starbucks was classified as the 8th best -paid CEO in the United States of America making $ 103 million dollars of profit ( Rushe, 2013). Hence, the question concerns that how Starbucks can predict its coffee customer fast accurate.

Micro and macro-economic marketing environment analysis: It is crucial to be aware and understand environment in which a company is operating in order to implement their strategies successfully. The micro environment strategies can be analyzed using in SWOT analysis and further completed with a macro environment study by doing a PEST analysis.

As Starbucks background, it can apply micro environment " a SWOT analysis" method, it must focus on the external factors since internal factors are rather analyzed in the core marketing strategy and extended marketing strategy and extended marketing mix. However, macro environment refers to everything external to the organization. So, it seems Starbucks can't necessarily fully control, only influence. Such as PEST analysis indicates political, economic, social and technological external environment factors. Such as certain political issues can raise since coffee beans are grown in developing countries and this could raise questions about the working conditions and child labor. Tariffs and import taxes could also influence the prices in stores as well as the country's economic recession or exchange rates change could threaten Starbuck's profits.

However, Starbucks internal strengths include that the development of new technologies and user friendly machines, such as home coffee machines, quality of beverages in other restaurants served are increasing and Starbucks should create Starbucks experience at home by manufacturing their own capsules machine with their coffee and tea. The emergence of social media is already used by Starbucks especially via Twitter where gift cards can be purchased and sent to friends ( Starbucks, 2014). There are Starbucks internal strengths to win its competitors, although, it can not control external environment factors to threaten its business.

Coffee drinking sale industry is a service marketing, positioning has received little attention from marketers, but is very useful in defining and modifying the tangible characteristics of the different kind of taste coffee product and its intangible perceptions.

As Starbucks, customers are buying an expensive product high quality (tangible ) every cup of different kind of taste coffee, but they also have the personalized in-store drinking experience enhanced by the trained employees, for example, the customer's name is written on the plastic cup their beverage will be served in ( tangible ), this helps Starbucks obtains the premium brand status and win competition.

Due to coffee drinking industry is a competitive business. In micro economy analysis strategy ( supply and demand). Nowadays, different coffee drinking service stores supply numbers are increasing. Although, it has limited supply numbers growth. Also, coffee drinkers' taste demand is changed quickly , who need to drink different kind og good taste coffees and they also considerate coffee stores' staffs service performance when they can let them to feel enjoyable to sit down the coffee shops to drink its coffee. Hence, Starbuck considers its employees' service performance issue. It concentrates on training its staffs to let its every coffee drinking client has unforgettable drinking coffee enjoyable experience in its any one coffee shop. It implies Starbucks employees' service behavioral performance can influence every coffee drinkers' positive or negative emotion to decide to choose to go to Starbuck to drink coffee again or choose another coffee shops to drink coffee. Hence, Starbucks employees' service behaviors must have relationship to influence its future coffee drinking client growth number. If it's employees can provide kindly service attitude to every coffee drinker, adds it can produce any kinds of good taste coffees, adds it can let coffee drinkers to feel it's every cup of coffee price is reasonable. Sum of all the factors, they can influence why Starbucks can earn more sale of its coffee shops in global different countries in short term successfully.

I conclude that Starbucks still needs to find different kinds of new taste coffee to satisfy different coffee taste clients' needs. Because coffee drinking market will have many clients who like to drink different kinds of coffee. If Starbucks can not increase to provide different kinds of new taste coffee to satisfy client individual drinking new coffee taste demand. Otherwise, other coffee shops can provide new unique different kinds taste of coffees to satisfy their drinking new taste coffee demands. Then, due to Starbucks limited supply of new taste coffee factor, it will have possible to influence its competitive ability in this competitive coffee drinking market.

In conclusion, it needs to consider how many coffee supply number is not the main factor to influence its success. Otherwise, how much different kinds of coffee taste supply is the main factor to influence its success because coffee drinkers can either choose to go to supermarkets to buy different brands of coffee to drink at home or choose to go to other coffee ships to drink the kinds of coffee taste which Starbucks can not provide to them to drink. So, satisfying coffee clients' different kinds of coffee taste demand will be one main successful key to Starbucks, it is not how many coffee number supply ( enough coffee number supply) factor to influence its success. It needs to find different kinds of new taste coffee to let clients to know and to have more coffee choice to drink to satisfy their drinking new taste of coffee needs. It reflects the new taste of coffee supply and the new taste of coffee demand micro economic theory to influence coffee consumers' drinking behavioral needs in this coffee drinking industry.

Micro economic assess the influence on location choices and growth performance consumption prediction.

Some economists indicate idea that seen central to the development of regional science at large and to economic geography and international trade theory. In this terms of economies of specialization increase returns to scale and in the case of regional science and economic geography, economies of localization and urbanization.

The questions concern: Can choose the best business location to attract consumption growth performance? Does the best destination attract consumption growth?

" Two cities attract trade from an intermediate town in the vicinity of the breaking point, approximately in direct proportion to the population of the two cities, and in inverse proportion to the squares of the distances of the intermediate town" ( Reggiani, 1998).

It implies some economists believe that geographic location choice factor can influence consumption growth. It is possible due to the location has many people are living. So, it brings many business chance, or the location is one the country's main in economic development location, it can attract many travelers choose to go to the location to travel. So, it has many travelling clients to prefer to consumer.

However, a smaller region can still attract consumption growth, if it had good transportation system. For example, a small region may not have its own university, but inhabitants may still have access to higher education. Elsewhere accessibility measures are also need in activity location models, where access ability is the way through which the quality of the transport system influences the land use.

So, it seems although the regional land is small size and far from cities, but if it can have good transportation system to provide any people to travel the small size regional land from outside cities. It is possible to bring consumption growth. However, some economists believe that distance influence relations in economics and economic geography in two ways: first, natural resources are distributed unevenly across space and second, distance separates various activities from each other. They apply " law of demand" to support their reasons.

In regional sciences, accessibility plays an important role for analyzing the distribution of economic cities and regional development. Within regional science, the attempt to predict and explain the distribution of economic activity has become known as economic geography. Research in economic geography attempt to answer the question: What forces cause geographic behavioral consumption? Some economists support the production function and into the interaction between transportation cost and plant level scale economies, this geographical factor will bring much geographical behavioral consumption. For example, accessibility of population is an indicator of market size for suppliers of products and services, whereas successful ability to GDP could be an indicator of the market size for suppliers of high level business services ( Spiekermannn and Wegener, 2007).

However, some economists argue that market potential is not necessarily the actual market. For example, since a person can't make the same purchase at two different locations. Hence, they believe that is one person has make purchase in one location far from whose home. Then, if he/she find another location which is close to whose home. The, he/she must not choose to buy the same purchase again, even he/she believe the seller's shop is close to whose home location. It implies that far location is not one factor to influence consumers to choose to buy the product if the consumer lines to buy the product. Even, the seller's shop is far away from whose home, he/she will still choose to drive whose car or catch transportation tool to go to the seller's shop to buy the product far away from whose home. Otherwise, if the consumer does not like the product, even the product seller's shop is close to whose home. Although he/she can walk to the shop to buy the product in short time. He/she won't choose to buy the product, due to who dislike the product. Hence, even close whose home, the seller product price is cheaper than the far away whose home, the another seller product price is higher than the similar or same product.

In conclusion, we have been downward trend of transportation costs of people, product and information to influence any geographical consumer behaviors. It implies that firms and people become less to restricted in their locational choices, it should lead to a greater homogeneity across regions. However, there are still great variation across geographical space in terms of incomes, cost of living, regional structure of production etc. different locational factors to influence regional consumption behavior in different countries.

# CHAPTER TWO

# Media economic methods to predict readers' behaviors in publishing industry

Media economics the application of economic theories, concepts and principles to study the macroeconomics and microeconomic aspects of most media consumption and industries, for academic lecturers, policymakers, and industry analysts. Media economics methods include how to apply variety of methodological approaches both qualitative and quantitative methods and statistical analysis, as well as studies using financial, historical and policy driven data.

Some economists define land, labor, and capital as the three factors of production and the major contributors to a nation's wealth. Can land, labor and capital be as three main factors of production any books, newspapers, magazines etc. reading products in publishing industry? Some economists believed price was determined by the costs of production, whereas marginal economists equated prices with the level of demand can be any books, magazines, newspapers etc. reading products prices is either determined by the cost of printing production or equated any one kind of these reading products with the level of reader' demand more.

The marginal economists contributed the basic analytic tools of demand and supply, consumer utility and the use of mathematics as analytical tools to develop microeconomics. Can apply the basic analytic tools of reader demand and the any one kind of these reading products supply and reading consumer individual reading need, utility and the use of mathematics as analytical tools to predict any kind of reading consumer numbers and reading interesting topic choice in media industry?

However, some economists also demonstrated that given a free market economy, such as in free publish industry, the factors of production ( land, labor and capital) were important in understanding the economic system. Can apply the factor of production , e.g. publishing book sale location ( land); publishing book salespeople sale experience ( labor); and attractive book printing quality (capital printing expense) to influence the publishing industry reading consumer reading habit or purchase book activities?

However, some economists suggested two important contributions: Analysis of monopoly and price discrimination and the market for labor will influence consumer number. Such as publishing case: Can analysis of which famous royalty publishing book sale firm to the most monopoly and then following its different topic of books sale price to evaluate whether how much every different topic of its similar book topic sale price to be higher to avoid reduce reader numbers, due to the not famous royalty book seller which similar topic book to the famous royalty book seller's prices are too higher than the famous royalty publishers' book prices?

Book salespeople individual sale experience and sale ability and book knowledge ( labor supply) influence the book publishing shop's reading clients buying decisions, such as the more experience book sellers can persuade many readers to buy the book store's books. Otherwise, the less sale experience book sellers can not persuade many readers to buy the store's books.

As the found in the field of economics, it became more refined, scholars began investigate many different economic concepts and principles to predict consumers behaviors, such as media reading customer. Nowadays, the media industries provides all of the elements required for studying the economic process. Content providers can offer information and entertainment, education etc. different topic books, magazine reading products which became the media publishing suppliers. Whereas, reading consumers and media advertisers formed the demand side of the media market.

The macroeconomic market conditions and the relationship among any media publishing reading product suppliers in various industries created microeconomic market conditions , e.g. publishing suppliers need logistic transportation service suppliers to help them to deliver books or magazines or newspapers etc. different kinds of reading products to book shops or magazine shops to sell every day. It can bring the logistic transportation service business to contribute social economic development.

Early media economists apply microeconomic concepts to examine newspaper competition and radio competition media industry. They predicted advertisement can help these both media industry to earn advertisement income to help other businesses to promote their products to let radio listeners and newspapers readers to know from these two media channel effectively. So, they believed that newspapers and radio extra income source can be provided advertisement service for other businesses, instead of radio audience income or newspapers reader normal income source. In addition to a number of book and edited volumes have contributed to the development of media economics to help them to predict consumer reading psychology.

How to apply media economic methods to predict media consumer's psychology? Some media economists believe the market structure-conduct performance model is as a tool for analysis, it has been widely used in the study of media markets and industries, such as book publishing industry. How to choose the attractive topic for every book product structure? They believe attractive book structure will help book structure firm to grow reader numbers. So, book topic and content factor is more influential to raise reader number more than cheaper book price sale factor.

In its most simply for the industries organizational model indicates that of the structure of the market is known, it allows explanation of the likely conduct and performance among firms. For example, in terms of market structure, the variables used for analysis include the numbers of sellers/ buyers, e.g. US publishing book market number of US book reading publishers/number of US book publishing sellers every year in US book publishing market; product differentiation, e.g. US different topic and content of electronic book or paper book product ; barriers to entry, e.g. economic recession, tariff book import tax, limitation of import book number etc. different external barriers factors to influence overseas ( foreign) book publishing import to US to sell their paper books ; cost structures, e.g. US book publishing firms need to spend how much printing expenditure to print high quality paper production of every paper book to sell and the degree of vertical integration, e.g. US book publishing firms how to choose middlemen to help them to sell books, e.g. themselves book publishing shops, other book retailers, themselves electronic book publishing website online platform sale channel or other book publishing sellers' websites online platform sale channel etc. different channels to sell the paper of electronic books to US readers. Hence, predicting the country' book market structure, it will have more confidence to evaluate book publishing competitors' effort and book sale price and how to design book content and topic to raise reading quality to let readers to feel much attractive to choose to buy the books from the book publishing shop.

Media economics research is in the sense that many different types of methods are used to answer research questions and investigate hypotheses. However, many economists accept to choose to apply any one of methods to predict media reader behavior, such as trend studies, financial analysis, econometrics and case studies.

Trend studies compare and contrast data over a time series. In assessing media concentration. Most trend studies use annual data as the unit of analysis. Trend studies are useful, due to their descriptive nature and ease of presentation and they aid in analyzing the performance of media companies and industries, e.g. study of changes in newspaper pricing and subscription costs.

Financial analysis is another common methodological tool used in media economics research. Financial analysis can take many different forms and use different types of data. The most common data include information derived from financial statements and the use of various types of financial ratio.

Econometrics involves the use of statistical and mathematical models to verify and develop economic research questions, hypotheses and theory.

Case studies represent another useful method in media economics research. Case studies are popular because they allow a researcher to gather different types of data as well as different methods. Case studies in media economics research tend to be very targeted and focused examinations.

What are forces to influence media industry development? There four forces consist of technology, regulation, globalization and sociocultural can influence media industry development. I shall indicate why these forces will influence media industry change in order media industry businesses need to consider s below:

Technology force: Because media industries are heavily dependent on technology for the creation, distribution and exhibition of various forms of media contents, changes in technology affect economic processes between and within the media industries. For example, many publishing book businesses choose to apply internet technology to help authors to publish electronic books sale. Due to it is popular to let online readers to study from internet, even they choose to pay visa card to buy electronic or paper books to read from internet sale channel. So, technology brings electronic book digital content and text and graphics digitally soon led to digital audio and video files to let authors to download their files to change to electronic books to publish to sell to electronic book readers to read from online channel. So, internet builds electronic book web sites to attract reading consumers to read from internet channel. They do not need to bring paper book to read. They only need to bring mobile phone or laptops to go to anywhere to read electronic books any time conveniently.

Regulation: If regulation is eliminated in publishing or media industry to any countries, the cross ownership rules would give publishing companies. The opportunity to acquire broadcast stations able cable systems within the markets, they serve, leading to the development of multi-media based companies offering content and advertising across multiple mediums.

Globalization can influence media industry development. Media products are often created with global audiences in mind, which is why so much content contains sex and violence. However, globalization of media content began with motion pictures and magazines, but then expanded into another media channels, e.g. television programming, VHS and DVD sales and rentals. These media publishing products' income are influenced by global audience entertainment choice.

Finally, it is socio-cultural force factor which can influence reader or media entertainment consumer industrial consumption behavior. Socio-cultural, such as the country's young people accept to like to read electronic books more than paper books reading behaviors. Then, it is the country's socio-cultural factor to influence the country's book buyers who prefer to pay visa card to buy electronic books to read from book store online website platform channel. It is electronic book reading cultural trend to influence the country young people reading behavior change . They will change their traditional reading habits to choose to buy electronic books to read from internet reading channel. So, online reading of electronic book method will be popular to the country and the country's paper book publishing shops ought consider to apply internet technology to develop their electronic book publishing business to let young people electronic book buyers to read electronic books from online channel conveniently.

Finally, all media industry players ought consider any technology development in order to predict readers' or media entertainment players' whose consumption behavior changes to avoid themselves publishing media businesses encounter fail in future one day.

Economic science or economic art methods predict consumer behavior

Economic is both a science and art. Economic is considered as science because systematic knowledge derived from observation, study and experimentation. An art is the practical application of knowledge for achieving definition ends. A science teaches us to know a phenomenon and art traches us to do a thing.

How to apply economic science or art method to predict consumer behavior? for example, there is a inflation US this year. This information is derived from positive science. The government takes certain fiscal and monetary measures to bring down to general level of prices in the country. The study of the monetary measures to bring down inflation makes the subject of economics as an art. Hence, as this case, if US government applies economic science or art method to predict this year will have inflation in US, then US government will attempt to avoid social general product prices to be raised, due to inflation influence. It aims to avoid US consumers reduce consumption desire in this year.

For another example, nothing could be more useful than water. But in much of the world waste is plentiful enough that another glass more or less matters little to a fresh water supply agent businessman. So, water is chap. But, if any offices buy bottle of glass fresh water to let employees to drink. It will bring advantages that they do not spend time to buy water to drink when they are working in the office time in any offices as well as employees do not need to heat water to drink to waste time to work in offices. So, the bottle of fresh drinking water supply agent is one kind of drinking water product monopoly fresh drinking water supplier to supply fresh drinking water to satisfy office employees who do not need to spend time to heat water to drink in offices. Hence, it is possible that replace other different kind taste of drink or office employees themselves heat water drink in offices. It is general office employees' drinking habits and drinking choice in offices popularly. So, the bottle of fresh drinking water supply agents will concentrate on selling their fresh drinking water to office employee customers only in global fresh drinking water consumption target market. The office employees must be fresh drinking water companies' main target consumers.

What is economic laws qualitative or quantitative method to predict consumer behavior? Law of economic are qualitative in nature. They are not exactly stated in quantitative terms. They tell the direction of change which is expected rather than the amount of change. For example, according to the law of consumer demand, the quantity demanded varies inversely with price, We don't say that 10% rise in price will lead to 30% fall in the customers' quantity demand.

What is economic merits of deduction method? This method is near to reality. It is less time consuming and less expensive. the use of mathematical techniques in deducing theories of economics brings exactness and clarity in economic analysis. The deductive method is highly abstract. It require a great deal of care to avoid bad logic or faulty economic reasoning. This method makes conclusions to predict consumer behavior, due to reliance on imperfect and correct assumptions.

It involves the process of reasoning from particular facts to general principle on the basic of experimentations, observations and statistical methods. In this method, data is collected about a certain economic phenomenon. There are systematically arranged and the general conclusions are drawn from them.

What are the advantages of inductive method to predict consumer behavior? It is based on facts as such the method is realistic. In order to test the economic principles, method makes statistical techniques. The inductive method is therefore more reliable, inductive method is dynamic. The changing economic phenomenon are analyzed and on the conclusions and solutions are drawn from them and this method also helps in future consumer behavioral investigations.

However, inductive method has weaknesses to predict consumer behavior, such as below:

It conclusions drawn from insufficient data, the generalizations obtained may be faulty. The collection of data itself is not easy task. The sources and methods employed in the collection of data differ from investigator to investigation. The result, therefore may differ even with the same problem and it is time-consuming and expensive to find data to predict consumer behavior changes.

How apply this method to predict general social consumer sources of income and consumption pattern when economic environment factor changes consumer behaviors? It should also be stressed that micro analysis plays other roles. First, it may serve to some macro data (any labor force by production sector or by skill category). Second, it can be used to estimate of key consumer behavioral consumption functions. For example, price and income elasticities can be estimated using data available in a typical householder budget survey. Third, in the case of tax reforms involving changes in exemptions or deductions is a model useful to estimate changes in effective tax rates changes how to influence consumer behavioral changes in society.

In conclusion, economists have proved macro and micro economic both methods have possible to be applied to predict consumer behavior when , how and why their consumption behavioral changing occurrence in order to manufacturers and product sellers or service providers can pre-make judgement to achieve the marketing strategies to avoid the number of client loss, due to marketing or economic environment changes to influence negative impact to consumer behavioral changes to influence the manufacturers' manufacturing products or the sellers' products or the service providers' service provision which number to be decreased.

Reference

Reggiani, A . (ed). 1998, accessibility, trade and locational behavior, Ashgate publishing ltd, England.

Rushe, D. (2013) " The 10 best paid CEO in America". The Guardian , 22 Oct, ( online). Available at:
http://www.theguardian.com/business/2013/Oct22/best-paid-chief-executives-america (Accessed: 3 May 2014).

Spiekermann and Wegener (2007), update of selected potential accessibility indicators. Final report, urban and regional research ( S&W), RRG spatial planning and geoinformation. ESPON. Available online
at http:// <www.espon.eu/mmp/online/website/ contentprojects/947/ 1297/file_2724/espon_accessibility_update-2006-fr_070207.pdf>, accessed on 1 July 2009.

Starbucks (2014) Our company available at http:// www. starbucks.com/about- us/company-information ( accessed: 3 May 2014).

# CHAPTER THREE

# How can artificial intelligent tools predict consumer behavior in vehicle market

Nowadays, many vehicle manufacturers hope their vehicles can attract to vehicle buyers to choose to buy their vehicles. However, there are many different brands of vehicles to provide to them to choose, so the vehicle market competition is very serious.

How to judge their different kinds of vehicle price which is reasonable acceptance to attract vehicle buyers to choose to buy the brand of vehicle manufacturers' any kinds of vehicles, e.g. fast speed sport style vehicles, comfortable and slow speed common cars, for four passengers common small size or more than four passengers common large car size? How to evaluate the vehicle prices issue is important factor to influence vehicle buyers' choices. Either if the brand of vehicle price is too high to compare brands, it will influence many vehicle buyers choose to buy other brands' vehicles or if the brand of vehicle price is too low, it will influence vehicle buyers feel this brand's vehicle's quality is worse to compare to other vehicle brands' similar vehicle products.

Thus, if the brand of vehicle manufacturers can predict how to design vehicles which can attract many vehicle buyers to choose to buy whose any vehicle products. What are future vehicle buyers' favorable vehicle styles? Then, the vehicle manufacturer can concentrate on manufacturing the kind style of vehicle products to sell already. It will reduce its vehicle manufacturing investment risk.

How to apply (AI) tools to predict vehicle buyers' behavioral consumption model? Whether artificial intelligent tools can predict automotive buyers' behavioral consumption model and predict future trend. In fact, automotive brands and dealerships are facing an increasingly competition when attempting to manually gathering the vast quantities of data required to create customer focused programs that increase retention, ultimately new sales and service automotive business. Building a based on that client's intrinsic needs and interests to any kinds of automotive vehicles at any given time. This is especially true in the automotive industry where the time span between purchases is measured in years. Because vehicle buyers would not like often to change their old vehicle to another new one. So, their decisions to buying another new vehicle, the time is usually after one year, even longer time. Hence, it seems any vehicles won't be frequent consumption products to the owned at least one vehicle family consumers (vehicle buyers).

Hence, how to predict vehicle consumers' taste or preferable which styles of vehicle choices issues is very important. If the vehicle manufacturers can not manufacture any attractive vehicles to sell easily in this year. Then, it will lose time, money in this year because it won't know when the owned least one vehicle users or non-owned any vehicle users who will decide to buy one new vehicle or change another new vehicle ensure. The different brand vehicle dealers will possible wait more than one year to attract them to buy their vehicles if their styles are not attractive to compare other brands of vehicle competitors.

However, artificial intelligence and machine learning can help any vehicle manufacturers to find solution to solve patterns in highly to solve patterns in highly complex data-sets that are beyond the capability of a human brain, and then building and automatically acting on the customer insights it generates.

Given the automotive customer need for individualized communications, this technology is positioned to become a critical component of any successful vehicle retailer's domestic or/and overseas vehicle markets. How can vehicle manufacturers and retailers use (AI) to enhance their vehicle marketing campaigns? How will (AI) affect their vehicle sale marketing strategy? What criteria would they use when selecting on (AI) solution?

Vehicle consumers today are able to quickly access different brands of vehicle information, research vehicle products and reviews, negotiate prices and compare one vehicle brand or retailer to another resulting of the brands of vehicle customers. At the same time, the rise of " big -data mining", wearable devices that track user's every move and preference and greater contextualization in advertising and social media has resulted in consumer expectations of individualized. Thus, it seems that (AI) tools can be used to gather " big-data" and then they can make human's mind to analyze how to design kinds of vehicles to satisfy vehicle buyers' needs.

As automotive vehicle marketers can apply (AI) tools to achieve messaging strategies to meet the needs of this new generation of informed vehicle consumers, using data from a variety of sources to move from a variety of sources to move from mass- messaging to more personalized messages aimed at particular vehicle buyer segments, e.g. fast speed sport vehicle buyer segment, slow speed comfortable small size or large size of buyer segment. However, when 90% of vehicle marketers believe having a single vehicle buyer view is important, only 6% have achieved it.

However, one of the main issues vehicle marketers facing is the lack of capacity to efficiently sift through and analyze the massive vehicle buyer amounts of data required to create vehicle buyer individualized vehicle customer experiences easily. This is especially difficult for automotive dealers, the long periods between purchase cycles, and the highly considered nature of the vehicle purchase means that each vehicle dealer needs to not only track a large number of potential vehicle customers for an extremely long period of time, but each of those vehicle customers will generate a huge amount of different kinds of vehicle behavioral consumption data as they research their next vehicle purchase. However, by choosing the right (AI) technological tools and programs , vehicle dealers can solve this big data gathering challenge into a major advantage.

For Forrester vehicle brand example, vehicle consumers have more power over the Forrester vehicle brand's reputation than ever before. Mayne, L. (2014) indicated that Forrester calls this new (AI) tools is the " age of the vehicle customer", a 20 year business cycle in which the most successful vehicle enterprises will reinvent themselves to systematically understand and serve increasingly powerful vehicle consumers. To win in this new age, Forrester declares companies must become vehicle customer obsessed and the only sustainable competitive advantage is knowledge and engagement with customers, such as (AI) gathering data knowledge.

Thus, the biggest challenge vehicle businesses currently face is not the collection of a large quantity of vehicle consumer data, but what to do with that data once they have it. Even at a large vehicle data research firm, the data sets are often too big for a single analyze, or even a team of analysts to sort through and draw conclusion from. However, enter artificial intelligence and machine learning , an efficient technology solution that can continuously find patterns in highly complex data sets that are way beyond the capacity of a human brain and then automatic drive action based on the customer insights is generated.

What is (AI) machine learning tool? Machine learning is a type of (AI) that learns from data and is not explicitly program. Think Amazon, face book. Machine learning serves up relevant content based on an individual vehicle purchase behavior and experiences. More simply, machine learning is a computer program that can learn relationships between data, subject those learnings to errors functions, and then learn from its errors. The program in effect, trains itself.

Lee, T. (2016) explained that "Thus, (AI) tools can learn deep a more advanced branch of machine learning inspired by how our brain's nervous function, has also been found to be especial effective in identifying patterns from data."

When this way sound is complicated from a vehicle dealer perspective, the implementation of a marketing program driven by artificial intelligence can take care of these tasks in an automatic vehicle fashion with little to no manual intervention required from the staff at time vehicle stores.

In practice at a vehicle dealership, the program will continue track vehicle customer behavior online, merging that data with any offline source ( like CRM or DMS data) and then analyze this aggregated vehicle buyer data set to predict what vehicle customer may be shopping for and what information they might like to relevance from different kinds style of vehicle design photos.

1.1 Why can (AI) be applied to predict consumer behaviors?

Artificial intelligence refers to complex in vehicle market, machine learning that posses the same characteristics of human intelligence and that have all our sense, all our reason and think just like human do. Besides, machine learning is the practice of using algorithms to collect and examine data, learn from it, and then make a determination or prediction about something in the world.

The machine is " trained" using large amounts of data and algorithms that give it the ability to learn how to automatically perform a task with increasing accuracy. Otherwise, deep learning is primarily based on artificial neural networks inspired by our understanding of the biology of human's brains.

Deep learning breaks down tasks in ways that enables machines to assist us with increasingly complex tasks, driverless cars, better preventive healthcare and more accurate product recommendation ( including vehicle recommendations). So, such as why (AI) technology can be applied to predict how vehicle consumer behavior changes to bring to judge whether vehicle consumer will like what kinds of vehicle styles next year. Then, vehicle manufacturers can gather overall vehicle consumer data to analyze and conclude the more accurate vehicle design direction for next year any new design vehicle manufacturing products.

Thus, (AI) machine learning can help vehicle manufacturers to solve how to design any new vehicle products challenge. A vehicle is both one of the most important and carefully considered purchases the majority of people will ever make in their lifetime. It is also a purchase that tends to be fundamentally tied to a person's identify and view of themselves. As the same time, vehicle consumers changing lifestyles result in changing vehicle needs, e.g. the young sport car enthusiast matures into the family driver.

Automotive dealers need to remember that vehicle customers and prospects are individual human beings with risk, complex and ever-changing lives factors, these factors will influence every vehicle consumer why who feels has vehicle purchase need, and how who choose to buy the first vehicle if who decided to buy the first vehicle.

The (AI) technological customer behavioral prediction tool seems to be the best vehicle salespeople in the world are those that know every one of their vehicle customers. Their likes and dislikes which style of vehicle design, preferences and changing tastes to vehicle choices. The capacity of the human brain, however, limits us from achieving this type of vehicle sales and frequent turnover at vehicle dealerships often results in the further loss of vehicle salespeople along with their vehicle customer relationships and knowledge. In this competitive vehicle environment, machine learning enables platforms to assist the vehicle sales team by tracking the vehicle consumer behaviors of each vehicle customer, learning and memorizing their preferences and predicting their future vehicle purchase needs.

Finally, I recommend that for a vehicle dealerships marketing platform to make their customer engagement efficient and fully-functional, I should be able to: applying (AI) tools to track every vehicle customer behavior across the web, connecting to a society of data sources, CRM, DMS, third-party, web vehicle brands, social email, click etc., aggregating and accurately cross-reference data from a variety of sources, leveraging this data to drive insights on a mass scale, as well as on an individualized basis, driving actions and automatically direct customer engagement via multiple channels based on where each customer is in their individual lifecycle.

How can (AI) provide businesses with better-informed decisions
I shall explain how (AI) technology can provide businesses with better-informed decisions to drive top-line growth, deliver meaningful experience for customers and smooth their path along the consumer journey. The widely understood definition of (AI) involves the ability of machines or computers to learn human thinking, reasoning and decision-making abilities.

A Narrative science study in 2015 year identified that (AI) was being used primarily in voice recognition, machine learning virtual assistants and decision support. This study also highlighted the many branches of (AI) and that techniques and their definition are used interchangeably. It is possible that (AI) can be used to gather big data , then to analyze to help businesses to predict consumer behaviors. For example, one of the most common techniques is machine learning, where algorithms are used to perform tasks by learning from historical data. Another growth branch of (AI) is natural language procession.

However, during 2017 year, search engines will begin to factor additional behavioral data into prediction of customer behavioral results, such as the user's history of searches and locations and previously captures conservations. Artificial intelligence will use this information to power predictive search results, e.g. predictive future consumer's choice behavioral processing for any kinds of businesses.

Predictive search will improve the quality of search results, and provide new insights into consumers' behavior and the moments which matter to them. Search will give recommendation into tailored how consumer individual choice in consumption process. Several of the largest online platforms already use machine learning to improve predictive consumer behavioral search results.

For example, Google's rank brain technology adds research by understanding the context in which the consumer has entered it. Over time, rank brain will learn further from user behaviors Amazon's DSSTNE ( pronouned destiny) learns from shoppers' purchasing habits and consumption behavior to offer better product recommend actions, which Amazon can offer before a consumer has entered anything into the search bar. However, this technology is not independent of human input. For example, Google engineers will periodically retain the rank brain system to improve the models it uses. For another example, in 2016 year , Apple computer revamped its photos app to allow consumers to search for specific items in the phots, they want to find, not just dates and locations. Each photo that an intelligent phone or intelligent pad user takes goes through 11 billion computations, so that photos can understand exactly what is the photography.

It seems that in future, (AI) machine learning will allow search to evolve even further. Search engineers will deliver refined recommendations to their business users and use less human input to predict consumers' needs. For IBM computer example, it indicated 90% of the data that exists today has been created in the last two years. This huge explosion of data gives brands the opportunity to quickly spot and react to the latest trends, fashion and fads among its clients and potential clients. This will allow companies to better engage with younger consumers, who gain influence access to the latest trends, and use the brands. They associate with to help define who they are as individuals. Thus, brands have to identify and make use of them before consumers move on, but the vast quantity of data available makes. This a resource-intensive task. For next example, Lesara, a based online clothes store, uses this machine learning to inform its product decision often gathering information from internal and external sources. When its trends -spotting shoes. Lesara has a range of over 20 styles and sells hundreds of pairs a day. It focus on giving consumers, the very latest trends allow Lesara to develop on average of 50,000 new items each year. It compared to 11,000 old items each year. Thus, (AI) brain seems to human brain to own analytical ability to predict consumer behaviors.

For another example, Lesara is one online clothes store, uses machine learning decisions after gathering information from internal and external sources. One of its most popular products, shoes with LED started life when its trend spotting software flagged up a blogger wearing similar shoes. Now Lesara has a range of over 20 styles and sells hundreds of pairs a day. Its focus on giving consumers the very latest trends allows Lesara to develop an average of 50,000 new items each year, compared to 11,000 for its competitor Lara. it seems (AI) machine learning can help Lesara business to predict what kinds of shoes design or style that shoe consumers will prefer choose to buy in future shoe market trend. Thus, Lesara can predict shoe consumers' taste successfully and it can manufacture many attractive style of shoes. (AI) machine learning can gather global past shoe consumer's shoe shopping experiences, then analyzes to make conclusion to give lesara recommendation successfully. This will make the experience more enjoyable for shoe consumers and allow Lesara to advert whose different new style or design of shoes to deliver them move relevant messages by understanding the context of the experience.

However, (AI) machine learning will have this risk who manufacturers need to concern if they applied this technology to predict consumer behavior. It is on sample consumers' privacy issue, in order to avoid complaint chance occurrence. However, machine learning can tie this data together to identify which f the billions of devices are being used by individual consumers. This helps brands understand how consumer engagement and actions can be attributed to different messages in different contexts and at different time. So, machine learning can help brands to build confidence to promote their products by any advertisement channels. When, this new (AI) machine learning technology can conclude how to design their products to be the most attractive, due to it has more accurate to predict consumer behaviors to compare human themselves prediction judgement effort. It seems that (AI) machine judgement effort is more accurate to compare to human judgment effort.

For example, google is moving away from cookies and using logged in data to track and make to users. It plans to expand the scope of the brand lift tool from online video. Thus, consumers are responded will to shippable context, finding it persuasive and easy to navigate by (AI) machine learning decision. For example, fashion brands can aggregate their You tub videos and blogs into a mobile context marketing experience, such as brand centric context into a personal shopping activity gives the shopper an experience, who are likely to remember and tell their friends about any new style of products design promotion from these internet advertisement channels after (AI) machine learning tools' styles of product design recommendation.

# CHAPTER FOUR

# What is (AI) deep learning techniques to forecast environment behavioral consumption

The (AI) deep-learning technology leads to performance enhancement and generalization of artificial intelligent technology. It influences the global leader in the field of information technology has declared its intention to utilize the deep-learning technology to solve environmental problems, such as climate change. So, it will help agriculture farming businesses can raise any plant food: vegetable, fruit, rice which grow up very easily if farmers can apply (AI) deep-learning technology to solve environment problems to influence their plant food grow. If the whole year seasonal change is very good and it is suitable for any plant food to grow in farming land easily, e.g. rain is enough and soil is enough for any plant food to grow in the farm lands. Then, fruit, rice, vegetable etc. agriculture businesses will have much beneficial attribution to global farmers.

The question is how to use deep-learning technologies in the environmental field to predict the status of pro-environmental consumption. We predicted the pro-environmental consumption index based on Google search query data, using a recurrent neural network ( RNN model). To certify the accuracy of the index, we compared the prediction accuracy of the RNN model with that of the ordinary least square and artificial necessary network models. For example, the RNN model predicts the pro-environmental consumption index better than any other model. we expect the RNN model to perform still better in a big data environment because the deep-learning technologies would be increasingly as the volume of data grows. So, deep-learning technologies could be useful in environmental forecasting to prevent damage caused by climate change to influence any rice, vegetable, tomato, potato, fruit etc. different plant food grow in any countries' farming land easily.

For South Korea example, over 800 government agencies spent 2.2 trillion Korea won on eco-products in 2014 year. However, green products are rarely purchased outside these agencies. This phenomenon occurs because there is a gap between consumer attitudes and behavior , that is environmental attitude is a major factor in decision making vis-a-vis the consumption of " green" food and services ( Jorea Ministry of Environment, 2015). Therefore, it is necessary to understand those consumer attitude, that will lead to sustainability-conductive behavior and consumption.


1 Environmental consumption prediction

Recently, many researchers have studied pro-environmental consumption and household indexes as well as suicide rate predictions using messages posted by internet users on Google trend, Tweets etc. channel. Whether can environmental consumption be predicted by (AI) deep-learning technological internet channel? How can impact the pro-environmental consumption attitudes of green policies? Korea scientists estimated pro-environmental attitudes using search query data provided by Google trend and confirmed through regression analysis, that pro-environmental attitude has a positive correlation with the pro-environmental attitude index. They also explained that environment-friendly attitude of residents plan an important role in policy making. In the past, most household consumption indexed were calculated through surveys, but (AI) deep-learning technological tool " big data" have recently gained research attention ( Lee et al. 2016).

It seems that (AI) deep-learning technology can help agricultural export countries' farmers , e.g. US, UK, Canada, New Zealand, Australia, Japan, China, India etc. they can predict environmental behavioral consumption to any rice, tomato, potato , fruit, vegetable etc. plant food consumers. The beneficial advantages to them include as below:

(a) Assuming they know their countries' weather, when it has less rain to cause drought or when it has more rain in any seasonal time in the year. They can choose not to grow any kinds of above these plant food to avoid loss.

(b) They can make any kinds of above these plant food price raising after their prediction of these bad seasonal time to cause their plant food shortage supply challenge. Because these plant food consumers' demand number is more, but the supply of these above plant food supply number is less. However, due to they had predicted when the bad seasonal time can not allow them to grow these above plant food before. So, they have enough time to grow many these above plant food number in predictive good seasonal time to prepare to supply to their plant food import countries' plant food consumers to eat. Thus, these predictive environmental consumption plant food export countries can raise their plant food price to sell to them. When, the other non-pre-predictive environmental consumption plant food export countries can not supply any one of those plant food to them to eat, due to the bad climate to cause them can't grow any one of these plant food to export to sell.

Thus, (AI) deep-learning technology can be applied to predict how to raise the plant food supply number in order to raise price to the import plant food countries consumers to eat, due to they feel difficult to buy these plant food to eat in the bad climate seasonal time in whole year.

(c) (AI) deep-learning technology can help climate scientists to find what reasons cause their countries; rain sudden increases or cause their countries' rain sudden decreases. After its gathering data analysis, it can assist climate scientists to find solution methods to attempt to control the rain level can be right falling down level to let agricultural export farmers who can grow their plant food to sell to agricultural import countries in whole year.

(d) The agricultural export countries' farmers can apply (AI) deep-learning technology to help them to choose whether growing which kinds of plant food in that whether climate time to earn more plant food consumption number more easily.

Due to the agricultural countries climate will often change, for example, tomato, potato, rice, fruit etc. plant food can be adapt to grow in more rain time, but vegetable can not be adapt to grow in more rain time. If farmers can apply this technology to predict when it will have move rain or when it will have less rain to fall down in their countries. Then, they can choose to grow which kinds of plant food number more, in the suitable seasonal climate time in order to raise plant food growing number productivities to supply to sell to satisfy any agricultural food import countries' demand effectively.

(e) (AI) deep-learning technology can help agricultural import countries to solve agricultural food shortage challenge in long term. When this technology can be popular to base applied by the agricultural plant food export countries. It will solve global agricultural food shortage challenge. For example, when one agricultural export countries' farmers can popular accept to apply this technology to predict when to grow which kinds of plant food more to rise number productivities to sell. e.g. vegetable, fruit, rice Besides another agricultural export countries' farmers can also accept to apply this technology to predict when to grow plant food, e.g. potato, tomato to raise number productivities to sell. Then, they can concentrate on growing the specific kinds of plant food in order to raise the specific plant food number productivities in every seasonal change time every month. Then, global agricultural plant food supply must be raised, due to these predictive environmental change farmers can know who ought grow which kinds of plant food to sell to raise number productivities.

How can apply (AI) digital channel to predict consumer behaviors?

(AI) digital channel can be applied to help businesses to evaluate whether how much the product price is the most attractive to persuade consumers feel it is the most reasonable price to sell. It helps consumers to feel which brands of products which ought change the price to let consumers to choose to buy the brand of product. It can be applied to predict whether how many consumer numbers can be increased or decreased when the brand of product's price is variable. It aims to give opinions to help any brand of product manufacturers or sellers to judge whether which price is the most reasonable to let consumers to accept to choose to buy the brand of product in popular.

Thus, (AI) price measurement technology can be preference to be applied online communication ecommerce and mobile phone internet platform aspect. As businesses can enter their past products prices data and past customer number data into computer or mobile. Then, (AI) price measurement technology can gather these data to analyze these product prices and past customer number to compare their prices variable changing range level to find their price variable difference to measure to make conclusion about every product's price variable changing will influence how many customer number increase or decrease changing to choose to sell their different kinds of products more accurate. Then, (AI) price measurement software will help them to analyze all past price variable changing data to compare whether which price range can let customers to feel it is more reasonable and attractive to influence them to choose to buy the product among different brands of product choice.

Because any product's price is one important factor to influence consumers to choose to buy the product, instead of quality, durability, shape, appearance, color, brand familiarity etc. factors. Any online businesses with a focus on Asia should considerate (AI) customer care, and virtual shopping experience, whereas is Europe and North America still value face-to-face and/or real human interaction over (AI) or virtual worlds.

For example, Amazon publish has applied (AI) price measurement technology to help authors to decide how much every different topic of e-book or paper book price, it can attract the largest number of readers to buy. Any one author only needs to type whose book name to Amazon publish author himself/herself Amazon website. Amazon publish (AI) price measurement learning machine will help them to auto-calculate and judge how much e-book or paper book price is the most attractive and the most reasonable in order to increase reader number to buy their e-books or paper books to read. So, (AI) online price measurement machine will gather past similar book names and past every similar book readers' reading times and the number of readers to give opinions to let every author to judge whether his/her very new e-book or paper book ought charge how much price to the e-book or paper book which can attract many readers to choose to buy. Although, it is not ensure that the e-book or paper book price must let readers to feel it is the most reasonable price to choose to buy in reader's view point. However, it has other factors to influence readers' choice to buy the e-book or paper book, e.g. whether the book content is attractive to public, the author's familiarity, the book's page is enough or not to satisfy readers to read etc. factors. But, instead of all these extra factors to influence readers to choose to buy the book to read. (AI) price measurement learning machine can real give opinions to every author to let them to judge the e-book or paper book different price range whether is too high to influence readers to choose to buy to read or tool low to influence readers feel it is possible poor content book to compare other similar content books. Thus, (AI) price measurement machine can help authors to predict every reader's reading behaviors or reading experience and reading habit from online channel in short time easily. The author only enter the book name to let

Amazon publish price measurement machine to check, it will follow past reader's reading habit and reading experience to judge whether the similar all book topic sale record to judge how much price is the reasonable price to attract many readers to buy the book.

Hence, (AI) can be applied to digital channel to help businesses to predict consumer behavior in the future. In the future, mobile/smartphone, laptop, desktop will be most frequent used ecommerce channels to develop online business. So, (AI) can be also applied to these platforms to gather data to make analysis to help businesses to predict consumer purchase behaviors popularly. Due to , ecommerce is popular to global, so digital online and instore channels can be one good channel to let (AI) learning machine to make platform to gather past every online consumer purchase ( buying) experience data to help businesses to build brand personality and having a responsible, positive impact on society.

To apply (AI) learning machine technology to understand customer online purchase behavior, it will raise business e-commerce successful chance: For example, (AI) learning machine can help businesses to gather data to analyze to determine whether short-term or long-term signals in the online consumer behavior that indicate higher purchase intents to let every online business to know. (AI) learning machine can find that online users with long-term purchasing intent tend to save and click through on more content. However, as online users approach the time of purchase their activity becomes more topically focused and actions shift from saves to searches from online consumption channel. Then, (AI) learning machine will further find that the brand product purchase signals in online behavior can exist weakness before an online purchase is made and can also be traced across different online purchase categories. Finally, (AI) learning machine synthesize these insights in predictive models of online user purchasing intent to the brand of product. Taken together, it's work identifies a set of general principles and signals that can be used to model online user purchasing intent across many online content discovery applications. Thus, (AI) learning machine can help online businesses to gather any online users' click online behaviors data to judge whether there are how many online users will choose to find their online business websites to make final decisions to buy their products from online channels. Then, it will give opinions to help the online businesses to let it to judge whether what are the important website factors will help its online business to attract many online consumers, e.g. designing unattractive website issue, online unattractive product photos issue, unclear website color issue, unclear website advertisement message, contents and words impressions issue, lacking image movement frequent attractive seeing issue etc. different website factors. Thus, online digital channel will be one good choice to apply (AI) learning machine to help businesses to predict consumer behaviors.

Can apply artificial intelligent learning machine " big data" gathering method to predict manufacturers' behavioral performance

In consumer view point, can they apply (AI) learning machine to predict manufacturers' behavioral performance to judge whether whose products are value to buy. Nowadays, (AI) and big data are reshaping the risk in consumer privacy. For example, consumers want to hide their willingness to pay just as firms want to hide their real marginal cost, and buyers have less favorable information, say a low credit shore, prefer to withhold it just as sellers want to conceal poor product quality. So, it implies that it is possible (AI) learning machine can help customers to gather any manufacturers' past sale performance, e.g. how many complaints or appreciation from clients, product quality etc. sale data to let consumers to make judgement whether it is value to buy to compare other competitors. So, it has risk to the poor product quality of manufacturers. Otherwise, it has benefits to the good product quality of manufacturers. It also implies all manufacturers' privacy is not protected or secret when (AI) learning machine is popular to be used to predict manufacturers' behaviors by consumers.

Information economists suggest that both buyers and sells have an incentive to hide or reveal private information, and these incentives are crucial for market efficiency. Data technology that reveals consumers type could facilitate a better match between product and consumer type, and data technology that helps buyers to assess product quality could encourage high quality production.

Thus, (AI) big data technology can also assist consumers to gather different manufacturers' data to compare what their advantages and disadvantages of their products are. Then, consumers can make comparison to choose which brand of product is the suitable to whom to buy in these more choice consumption market. (AI) learning machine will gather similar brand their products' data to analyze to make conclusion to let consumers know or feel to make final judge to find what advantages or disadvantages of these sample brands of similar products' comparison from internet. On the other hand, it means that manufacturers can gather consumers' past purchase behaviors or purchase experience from (AI) big data gathering method to record and analyze to give opinions to let manufacturers to know what reasons or factors influence consumers choose not to buy their products from internet.

(AI) big data gathering consumer behavior prediction method can give these benefits to manufacturers and consumers both, such as: New concerns arise because (AI) technological advance which have enables reducing cost of collecting, storing, processing and using data in mass quantities extend information beyond a single transaction. These advances are often summarized by the big data, it means charge volume of transaction-level data that could identify individual consumers by itself or in combination with the datasets.

The popular (AI) takes big data as in input in order to understand, predict and influence consumer behavior. Modern (AI) is used by legitimate companies, could improve management efficiency motivate innovations and better match demand and supply. But (AI) in the wrong hand, also allows the mass production of fraud and deception. Since , data can be stored, traded and used long after the transaction. Future data use is likely to grow with data processing technology, such as (AI) big data gathering consumer and manufacturer behavioral prediction method from internet channel.

Thus, future (AI) big data learning machine can also help consumers to choose the best brand of manufacturer's products among different brands of manufacturers products choice to compare their past sale performance from internet. They can apply (AI) big data statistic method to gather all different manufacturers' similar products past sale data to compare their advantages and disadvantages to make the best decision to choose to buy which brand of product is the most suitable to them to buy to use. It seems (AI) big data can also help consumers to predict any manufacturers' manufacturing behaviors or manufacturing performance whether they are improving their product quality or are deteriorating their product quality. Thus, (AI) big data tool is also important to help customers to predict future the different brands of manufacturer performance will have improvement in possible.

Thus, I believe that artificial intelligent "big data" gathering method can be suggested to be applied to attempt to predict consumer behavioral changes in global business environment, the reasons are as below:

On the consumer's beneficial hand, Consumers can apply this method to attempt to gather any global manufacturers data to be analyzed by this artificial intelligent learning system. Then, it analyzed all the different brands of specific similar product manufacturer' data to compare what are the range of the best past manufacturing history and sale data to the group of best manufacturers, and what are the range of the better past manufacturing history and sale data, and what are the range of the good past manufacturing history and sale data, and what are the range of the common past manufacturing history and sale data. Finally, the (AI) learning system will compare all the specific similar product, e.g. mobile phone or computer, television, car etc. different kinds of specific products of global manufacturers to conclude the result is such as whether which brands will be the best manufacturers to let the consumer to buy the television or mobile phone or computer or car etc. different kinds of products. It can make more accurate judgement to compare general human's phone or questionnaire surveys investigation method, newspapers, television, radios, internet searches etc. different manufacturing news or data gathering channels to find which brands are the most worth confidence to consumers to choose to buy the specific product in the global consumption market.

On the manufacturers' beneficial hand, manufacturers can apply (AI) data gathering method to predict consumer emotion and buying behavioral changes more accurate. For example, the vehicle manufacturer, it plans to gather data to predict potential driving fast speed sport vehicle consumers' preferences trends in order to make the accurate judgement how to design its sport vehicles to attract many sport vehicle buyers who will choose to buy it's brand of any driving fast speed sport vehicles. It can attempt to apply (AI) intelligent learning system to gather global different brands of sport vehicle data concerns that all past driving fast speed sport vehicle buyer's preference of sport vehicle design. Then, the (AI) intelligent learning system gather global different brands of driving fast speed sport vehicle which had ever been purchased by the different country's driving fast speed sport vehicles consumers. After, it can compare divide the range of similar driving fast speed sport vehicle design and similar price to be different groups. The (AI) intelligent learning system can attempt to follow the past number of different brands of driving fast speed sport vehicle buyers to calculate how many driving fast speed sport vehicle buyers who choose to buy the brand of driving fast speed sport vehicle as well as it will analyze and make judgement to find whether the cheaper price reason attracts the different countries sport vehicle buyers choose to buy the brand of driving fast speed sport vehicle or the attractive design reason attracts the different countries sport vehicle buyers choose to buy the brand of sport vehicle or fast speed reason attracts the sport vehicle buyers choose to buy the brand of sport vehicle.

For example, although some brands of driving fast speed sport vehicle manufacturers' prices are very high, but they can still attract global many sport vehicle consumers to buy. Whether all sport vehicle's attractive design is the main factor to influence them to buy or whether it's fast speed is the main factor to influence them to buy or whether it's safe confidence it the main factor to influence them to buy or it's familiarity brand is the main factor to influence them to buy. (AI) intelligent learning system will attempt to make judgement and analysis to conclude whether the attractive design factor is the main factor to influence many sport vehicle consumers to choose to buy the brand of sport vehicles.

Otherwise, for another example, although some brands of driving fast speed sport vehicle manufacturer's prices are low, but they can not still attract many global many sport vehicle consumers to buy. Whether all vehicle's unattractive design is the main factor to influence them choose not to buy their fast speed driving sport vehicles or whether the unsafe factor is the main factor to influence them choose not to buy their fast speed driving sport vehicles or whether unfamiliarity brand is the main factor to influence many consumers choose not to buy their fast speeding sport vehicles.

Thus, when (AI) learning system had helped the fast speed sport vehicles manufacturer to gather all different brands of fast speed driving sport vehicle's past sale data and price data, design of different sport vehicle, e.g. color choice, method of style, comfortable chair styles and chair sizes and what kinds of steel material to manufacture the sport vehicles data and driving safe and accident occurrence data and the data concerns what reasons of the past complaint to brand of sport vehicle manufacturer from its sport vehicle buyers. Then, it can make more conclusion to give more accurate opinions whether which brands of fast speed driving sport vehicle manufacturer(s) whose sport vehicle design is the main factor to attract consumers choose to buy its any driving fast speed sport vehicle products really. Thus, it seems that it can make more accurate judgement to compare television survey, questionnaire survey to gather data concerns how to design the fast speed sport vehicle to attract consumers to choose to buy the sport vehicle manufacturer's planning sport vehicle products. I believe that

(AI) learning system can help the sport vehicle manufacturer to make more accurate conclusion or judgement how to design its fast speed driving sport vehicles to attract it's consumers more easily.

Reference

Korea Ministry Of Environment. Public Organizations spend 2.2 Trillon Korean Won To Purchase green Products in 2014; Ministry Of Environment: Sejoung, Korea, 2015.

Kuvayev leonid, (1996) Predicting financial markets with neural networks.

Mayne, Lonnie. " Evolve of die in the age of the consumer". Entrepreneur, N.P. , 16 Apr. 2014. web of Oct. 2016.

lee, D.; Kim, M. ; Lee, J. adoption of green electricity policies: Investigating the role of environmental attitudes via big data-driven search-queries. Energy policy 2016. 90, 187-201.

Lee, Terrence, " Tech in Asia-connecting Asia's startup system " Tech. in Asia- connecting Asia's startup ecosystem, N.p.,4 July 2016.

# CHAPTER FIVE

# What is artificial intelligent financial market variable prediction and human's brain similar function

How can apply artificial intelligence predict future oil prices variable? How does this work to begin with and why have human not been replaced by this technology yet? Firstly, I shall assume a sense of the mindset of people trying to solve similar problems in financial market price variable issues.

In common, the efficient market hypothesis is the idea that all relevant information on a financial asset always is incorporated into its price. The only thing that can change the price is new information which is unpredictable by its nature. Whether insider information is incorporated into the product's price or not but they are similar in the sense that at least public information is considered to be incorporated into the product's current price.

In financial market industry, some mutual fund managers are expected what return if these managers would have no relevant knowledge at all. Fundamental analysts try to examine companies, analyzing its financial statements and evaluate it, investing it seems to be wrongly priced, assuming it will be correctly valued in the future. Even, a technical analyst might aim at predicting investors emotional response from negative news on a specific stock, trying to make a profit from predictable patterns.

(AI) manybe it is possible to create machines that can accomplish as complicated goals as humans, and in this process also be able to define what intelligence is. It is a supercomputer and eventually simulate a human brain to understand it better. (AI) has been used for attempts to achieve with various success, such as one of the methods is to think human like. This is sometimes desirable and sometimes not. For example, one way humans might think which is not desirable when attempting to achieve (AI) is, what is known as the gambler.

Imagine a scenario where a person flips a fair coin ten times, and that the first none lands head, many people would say that the probability is higher that the next flip will land tails, but it is not. When those heads already have been flipped, the probability of the next flip landing tails is still 0.5=50%. That is an example of human thinking many wishes to avoid instead when creating (AI). Human expect it can calculate the chance or possibility of flip landing tails more accurate.

An artificial neural network is s computational structure inspired by neural networks naturally occurring in living organizations. The human brain has many biological neural networks which in themselves consist of connected united neural networks that send electrical impluses to each other puts depending on the input. The motive for neuroscientists for this replication is to understand biological, neural networks better. So, it is possible that (AI) can be invented to own human's similar living organisms, such as neural network in brain.


6.1 How to apply artificial intelligence to predict
financial market variable behavior

A financial market means financial instructments are traded. A financial instrument is a term for any tradable financial contract. For instance , a share in a company , every stock of the same type in the same company are equivalent. Generally, various financial markets were targeted by researcher trying to forecast them in order to achieve to earn profit between buying and selling every share transaction.

However, (AI) technological prediction of financial market variable behavior when the share price will rise up or fall down more accurate. It needs have these data inputs and to what market the technique was applied , e.g. ( exchange rates, stock indices). Furthermore, data also include what input variables that were used ( technical analysis variables, fundmental analysis variables etc).


6.2 What techniques that were used and whether or not was a trading system? What is surveying stock market forcasting techniques?

(AI) techniques can apply survey method to gather data, then to predict whether what economic problems will occue to evaluate when share price will change either to be risen up or fallen doen more accurate. Thus, (AI) is performed a survey on machine learning techniques that had been applied to predict stock market movement.

6.3 What problems do (AI) surveying stock market prediction technique encounter?

The problems may include as below:
Firstly, it is a time-consuming problems. (AI) survey stock market prediction technique must need spend much time to gather different industry' past financial market stock movement data in order to achieve more accurate future share price variable prediction. Seocndly, organizations need to employ the owning (AI) financial market surveying stock market prediction technique professonals to help them to do every time gather data tasks for every company's past share price movement history data.

6.4 What is a software engineering systematic mapping method?
It is a defined method to build a classification scheme and structure a software engineering field of interest. The analysis of results focuses on frequencies of publications for categories with the scheme. So, every time (AI) surveying search field can be determined. The primary goal of the method is to give an overview of every past share price investigation research can predict future share price movement for the firm.
Forecasting of stock market using artificial
neural network

Nowadays, shareholders like to apply (AI) technology to forecast stock market return is gining more attention. Shareholders believe (AI) systems are highly sensitive, dynamic, a periodic, complicated and its neural networks are effective in learning, such non-linear chaotic systems because they make very few assumptions to predict the movement of share price more accurate than human's judgement. Many researchers and practioners have proposed many models using various fundamental, technical and analytical techniques to give a more or less exact prediction to stock price movement.

1 How does shareholders apply (AI) neural network to predict share price movement?

The shareholders' technical analysis will concentrate on using share price, volume, and open interest statistical charts to predict future stock movements. Apart from these commonl used methods of predicton. Some traditional time series forecasting and open interest statistical charts to predict future stock movement. Apart from these commonl used methods of predicton. Some traditional time series forecasting tools are also used for the same. In time series forecasting, the past data of the prediction variable is analyzed and modeled to capture the patterns of the historic changes in the variable. This models are then used to forecast the future shares movement prices.

2 What is (AI) neural network system?

A neural network is a massively parallel distributed processor made up of simple processing unit, which has a natural propensity for storing experiential knowledge and making it available for use. Neural networks have ability to derive meaning from complicated or imprecise data. They are used to extract ptterns and detect trends that are tool complex to be noticed by either humans or other computer techniques ( Kuvayev. L., 1996).

3 Why is (AI) neural network better than shareholder himself/herself judgement to predict share price movement?
I shall indicate with an exmaple to explain two analysts consideration, A and B, covering company (C). Imagine that analyst A has estimated that this (C) company will achieve earning per share (EPS) of $1 for the first quarter of its fiscal year and $4 for the entire year, when analyst B has estimated that the same company will achieve EPS of $1 for fiscal quarter one and $4 for the entire year. So, analysts A & B can predict the share price movement accurately. Analysts other than A and B cover company (C), and the median EPS estimate for the (C) company's first fiscal quarter is also same to analyst B's estimation $1.
Now image that (C) 's earnings announcement for the quarter reveals that its actual first quarter EPS was $0.9, proving that the estimate of analyst A and B have off in the wrong direction. One average , we find the extreme analyst A adjusts his EPS estimate for the remaining quarters less in the direction of the earnings surprise than the analyst B with a forecast matching. For instance, analyst A might update his EPS estimate for the fiscal year to $4.2 from $4.4 , while analyst B might update has EPS estimate for the fiscal year to $3.8 from $4. So, it seems human's estimation is much

difficult and complicate to compare artificial neural network analysis to predict share price movement.

As this case , analysts in this situation as " incorrect and of consensus analysts" and it refers to their forecasts as " incorrect out-of-consensus forecasts". We don't focus on analysts whose quarterly earnings deviate from the median quarterly forecast in the same direction as announced quarterly earnings. Since analysts in this situation have a strong rationale for maintaining their on a company (C).

However, we find that the type of descriptive above reduces the accuracy of analysts' forecasts, suggesting that our results are not driven by superior private information. Hence, artificial neural networks can help shareholders to gather all past share price movement data concerns company(C). Then, it will attempt to analyze to make more accurate prediction about the company (C)'s share price movement in one month, half month, even shorten time till to one day company (C) 's share price movement situation more accurately to compare every analyst individual share price judgement for company (C) share price movement prediction.


4 Why can artificial neural network machine system make more accurate share price movement prediction more than human analysts?

The reasons are because an analyst who frequently changes individual mind about a company as lacking an understanding of the company. On the other hand, an analyst who sticks to an out-of-consensus view many receive attention from investors because of whose individual unique perspective and may also be more credible the next time he/she makes an out of consensus forecast.

Otherwise, artificial neural network machine system won't be influenced by shareholder investors' view points of past wrong different companys' shares buying and selling experience influences. So, artificial machine only makes every different companys' shares movement prediction by the company whole all years' share price movement gathering data to conclude to make more accurate estimate to judge whether what share price range to be risen or fallen down in this month, or in this week , even tomorrow short term more accurate prediction than human analysts' prediction.

# CHAPTER SIX

# Main barriers influence artificial intelligence consumer behavioral prediction

In future, it is possible that these barriers will influence how to apply (AI technology) to predict consumer behavior in success. The barriers may include: Lacking of a (AI) digital data gathering vision and strategy, lacking of efficient workforce readiness, (AI) technology constraints., non reaching (AI) consumer behavioral prediction mature stage, time and money and resource constraints, law and regulations prohibition to develop (AI) consumer behavioral prediction bug data gather technology.

However, the recommendation of solutions to attack the barriers to influence artificial intelligence consumer behavioral prediction not success, it may include gaining employee buy in to participate and develop (AI) consumer behavioral prediction technology, making customer experience to a concern (AI) big data gather questionnaire investigation, providing compensation, training to employees in order to achieve (AI) consumer behavioral big data questionnaire investigation research digital technological goals and strategy, task senior leaders manage any (AI) digital big data gather technology changes, putting policies and (AI) big data gather digital technology in place to support a fully remote, flexible workforce in any (AI) digital big data gather questionnaires research projects, teaching all employees how to code/understand (AI) big data gather consumer behavioral prediction software development, appointing a chief (AI) officer to manage any (AI) big data gather customer behavioral prediction projects and automate everything and encourage customers to attempt experience to self-service and (AI) big data gather questionnaire research to earn beneficial consumption aim after they gave feedback to any (AI) digital questionnaire researches. So, in the future, the (AI) digital big data questionnaire researches can include these industries surveyed, such as automat m financial services, public healthcare, private healthcare, technology, telecoms, insurance, life sciences, manufacturing, media and entertainment , oil and gas, retail and consumer products etc.

Hence, in the future, any of these industries can attempt to apply (AI) digital big data gather technology to predict how and why consumer behaviors will change in order to avoid reducing consumer number threat occurrence.

(AI) digital data gather technology predicts food consumer behavior's main barriers

What are the main barriers to food industry? When the food manufacturer applies (AI) big data gather technology to predict food consumer behavior? The barriers include that the food manufacturer / provider needs to decide whether when the right time is applied to the right (AI) digital big data prediction tool channel to find the right food consumers to be chose to full food consumption satisfactory questionnaires, how to gather multi-class food consumption classifiers on real-world food consumers transactional data from the food sale domain consistently to show the critical numbers of different kinds of food items at which the predictive performance most accurate? So, any food manufacturer / provider's advanced in (AI) digital data gather warehousing and management technologies can provide that opportunities for food business to enhance long term relationship with the food providers' clients.

However, food industry's (AI) digital data gather aims to improve food customer product targeting, increase food customer loyalty and food purchase probability to the food supplier. To effective identify, understand and satisfy the needs of their food customers, the food suppliers need to develop the right (AI) digital questionnaire questions and find the right food customers to fill every right questions from every digital questionnaire at the right time through the right channel.

Above of all these, they will be the barriers when one food supplier expects its (AI) digital data gather questionnaires which can conclude the most accurate prediction concerns any kinds of consumer food product choices. So, such as (AI) digital data prediction model, it is needed to incorporate into the food market segmentation, food customer targeting, and food challenging decisions with the goal of maximizing the total food customer lifetime. For example, (AI) big data gather transaction data is reasonable and accurate for building predictive models. Transaction data can be electronically collected and readily made available for data mining in lot quantity at minimum extra costs.

Suggestion to apply (AI) prototypes of food customer profiles method to predict food customer behavioral changes. Prototypes of food customer profiles mean to be extracted from the discovered bins and multi-class classifies models are built using those prototypes. The learned models can than be used to predict the class of food customer profiles ( e.g. restaurants, school canteens, supermarkets etc. food suppliers) based on their food purchases. The approach is validated on the case study of a food retail and food service company operating in food and beverages market.

So, a food customer profile, it is a description (AI) data gather tool will record every of food customer using available information, which help in understanding their background and food consumption behavior. (AI) data gather tool can well develop every food customer profile, every food customer data is essential in food market analysis as they aid food suppliers in saving time and money by highlighting the real potential food consumers whose needs are to be met rather a range of individuals.

So, (AI) data gather tool can record every food consumer profile and every can be factual or behavioral food consumption. A factual food customer profile consists of a set of characteristics for (AI) big data gather record, e.g. demographic information , such as food customer name, gender, birth date, when a behavioral food customer profile consists of what the food customer is actually doing and is usually derived from (AI) digital transactional data gather record.

So, (AI) big data gather record's every behavioral food consumer profile can be much stronger predictor of the future food supplier consumption choice actions of a food customer. Furthermore, the food supplier's (AI) all past food consumer information that make up demographically based all past food customer profiles are expensive to acquire when the information for the food suppliers' past every food consumer food consumption behaviors. Moreover, food customer profile can be recorded to make real food purchase every time. So, when the food supplier finds the past food consumer's record from (AI) big data gather tool. Then, it can make more accurate judgement whether past every food consumer has chose to buy its food to eat how many times every year in order to predict whether its every past food consumer will choose to buy its foods how many times next year in possible. If the next year, its every past food consumer's consumption time to the food supplier is less than its current year consumption time. Then, the food supplier can attempt to find whether what factors to cause the past food consumers do not choose to increase food purchase times to the food supplier in current year. The factors may be possible be the food supplier's food prices are raised, food quality or taste is poor, the different kinds of food supply is shortage challenge, the food supplier's consumers lose confidence to buy the food supplier's foods to eat, when (AI) big data gather tool can help the food suppliers to find what the main factors to cause the past food consumer number to be reduced in order to predict how future food consumers' behavioral changes will be influenced from the food supplier's competitors in the global food supply market. Hence, (AI) big data gather tool can help every food supplier to attempt to find what the main factors to case the food supplier's food consumer number to be reduced as well as it can help the food supplier to predict how the food supplier's potential ( past not every purchase its any food consumers) food consumers who can be persuaded to choose to buy its foods to eat by learning what the main factors influence.

In conclusion, (AI) big data gather tool can help the food supplier to find what the main factors influence its past food consumers do not choose to buy its food more times or find what the main factors will attract its potential ( not ever buying its foods consumes) food consumers to choose to buy the food supplier's foods to eat.

The challenges of (AI) big data gather shaping
the future of retail for consumer industries

Another challenge of (AI) big data gather is that how to shape the consumer behavior to let business owner to feel or know or predict. It means that how it express it's conclusion or opinion for every consumer behavior after it had gather all big data in any data gather period, e.g. three months, half year or one year consumer shopping model data gather period.

Because every kind of industry, consumers will continue to demand price and quality change , with a wide range of convenient fulfilment options among of different kinds of products or services supply. Overall, the (AI) big data gather procedure gives opinion concerns every time retail experience will become more exciting, simple and convenient, depending on the consumer's ever-changing needs. So, I believe that (AI) big data gather every conclusion or result will be different, due to consumer's price and quality demand will often change to every kind of product or service supply in retail industry. So, how to shape (AI) big data gathering's analytical conclusion or result more clear. I shall recommend organizations need to build great understanding of and a stronger connection to increasingly empowered consumers before they plan and implement how to apply (AI) big data gather tool to predict consumer behavior as below:

Firstly, (AI) is empowered by technology, the consumer is redefining value. The traditional measures of cost, choice and convenience are still relevant, but not control and experience are also important. Globally, consumers have access to more than 2 billion different products choice by a wide range of traditional competitors and dynamic new entrants, all experimenting with new business models and methods of client engagement.

As choice increases, loyalty becomes more difficult familiarity and the consumer becomes more empowered. Businesses will have no choice and constantly innovate and disrupt themselves by meeting new technologies of high standards and expectations of consumers. So, (AI) data gather tool will need to follow different target group of consumers' needs to follow their different kinds of product design or style choice preferable to gather data in order to conclude the different target groups of consumer behavior to give opinion more clear and accurate to let businessmen to understand more clear how its customers' behavioral choice trend in the future half month, even to two years period.

Secondly, businessmen need to adopt changing technologies rapidly. Technology will be the key driver of this retail industry. Industry participants will only success if they have a clear prediction to focus on how to using technology to increase the value added to consumers. They must , however, do so will I realistic assessment of their costs and benefits. Hence, (AI) big data gather technological tools will need to design to help them to gather data efficiently by these ways, such as the internet of things ( IOT), artificial intelligence (AI) machine learning, augmented reality (AR)/virtual reality (VR), digital traceability. So, future (AI) big data gather tool are predicted to be most influential customer behavioral positive emotion changing tool for retail , due to their widespread applications , ability to drive efficiencies and impact on labor in order to impact consumer behavior changing effort from negative emotion to positive.

Thirdly, (AI) big data gather tool is an advanced data science of consumer behavior predictive tool. Businesses will have to bring the journey from simply collecting consumer data to using it to scale and systematize enhanced decision making across the entire value chain. When focused on their business goals, industry players should not lose sight of the impact that future capabilities and transformative business models may have on society.

However, (AI) big data gather tool will encounter these challenges when any business plans and implements to apply it to predict consumer behavior in retail industry. The challenges include that as below:

1. The high cost and difficulty of implementing new technologies . The (AI) big data gather tool needs capital and capabilities to be designed to implement to be applied to different retail industry users. so, expensive barriers to innovation, an organization and the skillsets of its people to support a new design of (AI) big data gather tool, highly digital technology may be required.

2. Slow pace of cultural change. Consumers need to adapt or accept (AI) new technology consumption model in the traditional retail industry. The rate of change is outpacing the ability of businesses to keep up. (AI) big data gather tool needs to be designed to adopt in new or evolved business model requires, in most cases, a new level of customer behavioral predictive machine operation will impact to influence any retail businesses' consumer behavioral changes at a minimum, an organization's structure, capabilities, culture and decision making. If the retail business expects to apply (AI) big data gather tool to predict how to change its consumer behaviors and how their consumption behaviors will tend to change in order to achieve to change their positive emotion from negative emotion before they choose to buy its product or consume its service in success.

Challenge to using (AI) neural networks to predict customer behavior from big data gather tool

(AI) big data gather tool will encounter the challenge: How can predict customer behavior be represented as sequential data describing the interactions of the customer with a company or an (AI) data gather system through the time, e.g. these interactions are items that the customer purchase or views ? So, every customer data gather , (AI) needs to spend time to analyze how and why to cause whose consumption behavioral choice. It is too difficult matter or judgement for (AI) learning. So, (AI) needs to spend time to learn how to analyze every customer's shopping behavior or actin in order to gather all different consumers' past shopping action information in order to help business owners to predict future its potential customer shopping behavior how to change more clear and accurate prediction.

(AI) big data gather tool needs to learn to know that how to judge every customer interaction likes purchases over time can be represented with sequential data. Sequential data has the main property that the order of the information is important. Many (AI) machine learning models are not suited for sequential data, as they consider each input sample independent from previous ones. Therefore, at the end of the sequence, (AI) big data gather learn machines need to keep in their internal state of every customer purchase data, kind of product or service, price , whole year consumption times form all previous inputs, making them suitable for this type of data.

However, consumer behavior can be represented as sequential data describing the interactions through the time. Examples of these interactions are the items that the user purchases or views. Therefore, the history of interactions can be modeled as sequential data, which has the particular trial that an incorporate a temporal aspect. For example, if a user buys a new mobile phone, who might purchase accessories for this mobile phone in the near future or it the user buys a electronic book or paper book , he might be interested in books by the same author. Therefore, to make accurate predictions is important to model this temporal aspect correctly. To solve this predictive challenge of consumers to buy the product. One count the number of purchased products of a particular category in the last N days, or the number of days since the last purchase.

So, the (AI) big data gather designers can attempt to produce a feature vector which can be fed into a machine learning algorithm such as " logistic regression" will be the main feature and function to any (AI) big data gather machine to learn how to apply this " logistic regression" function or feature to predict any customer behavioral change for any product purchase or service consumption to the (AI) predictive consumer behavioral business users. Every different kinds of product purchases or services consumption will be needed to design " different model of logistic regression" in order to follow the kind of business to predict whose consumer purchase or service consumption behavior to predict more accurate.

Challenges of artificial intelligence, algorithms technology and machine learning impact to consumption market

Markets have played a key role in providing individuals and businesses with the opportunity to gain from trade. If (AI) big data gather tool can predict how to change potential customer behavior in success. The challenges to consumers will face that the overall market consumption model will be dominated by the businessmen only. So, it is not fair or reasonable to consumers, because (AI) big data gather tool has controlled or dominated all consumers' minds and it has predicted how and why every kind of product or service consumer shopping model or consumption behaviors how will change.

It will bring this questions: How can market designers learn the characteristics necessary to set optimal, or at least better, reserve prices after they had gather all data to conclude the analytical results of their consumers behaviors how will change? How can market designers better learn the environments of their markets?

In response to these challenges, artificial intelligence (AI ) and machine learning are important tools for market design. For example, retailers and marketplaces , such as eBay, Amazon and many others are mining their vast amounts of data to identity patterns that help them create better shopping experiences for their clients and increase the efficiency of their markets. By having better prediction tools, these and their companies can predict and better manage dynamic consumption market environments. The improved forecasting that (AI) and machine learning algorithms provide help marketplaces and retailers better anticipate consumer demand and producer supply as well as help target products and activities for segmented markets. Another important application of (AI) 's strength in improving forecasting to help markets operate more efficiently is in electricity market example. To operate efficiently, electricity marker makers can attempt to apply (AI) machine learning tool to follow every household family electricity consumers' past electricity consumption record to judge ( predict) how it will be every family's forecasting in the year.

An inaccurate forecast in the electricity supply and demand that can dramatically affect electricity market bad supply outcomes causing high variance in electricity charge prices or worse, blackouts. By better predicting every family's electricity demand and supply , electricity market makers can better allocate power generation to the most efficient power sources and maintain a more reasonable electricity stable charge market. Any example is design market, the application of (AI) algorithms to market design are already widespread and diverse.

(AI) algorithms technology , it is a safe that (AI) will play a growing role in the design and implementation of market over a wide range of applications. The challenges are that how (AI) can guarantee accurate to predict when and why and how consumer behavioral changes to any retail industries. In fact, retailers will need to discover the value that (AI) can bring to what benefits to influence their customer behaviors.

In the future, (AI) will bring their benefits to influence customers to build positive emotions to any retailers in these aspects as below:

1. Future (AI) big data gather tool will be an area of compute science that deals with giving machines , the ability to seem like they have human intelligence. In short, it is the power of a machine to copy intelligent human behavior. For example, machine learning algorithms are being integrated into analytics and customer relationship management platforms to uncover information on how to better serve customers, chat bots have been incorporated into websites to provide immediate service to customers.

2. (AI) adoption continue to rise with chat bots taking the lead. Due to increasing ease of deployment , instant availability and improved quality, chat bots will become more and more common to manage customer service queries and to make intelligent purchase recommendations. Also, retailers can engage this kind of technology to answer continue questions and supplement customer support with chat-based shopping experience. So, (AI) and declines personalized, customized and localized experiences to customers.

(AI) will be applied across the entire retail product and service cycle, firm manufacturing to post-sale customer service interactions. Hence, retailers can use (AI) to its fullest potential will be also to influence purchases in the moment and anticipate future purchases, guiding shoppers towards the right products in a regular and highly personalized manner.

3. (AI) technology can rise the conscious customers. Customers are demanding an increased interest in the ethical practice of the brands they buy from. Todays, customers have a well-developed sense of what is solely intended to drive sales. This has lead to a rise in consumers ho make

values based judgements about what to buy and where to shop. These consumers believe their purchase habits have an impact on the world. To win customers, retailers need have good conscious to predict consumers' desire. Future, (AI) data gather technology will be a good consumer behavior predictive tool to predict about for years will now become customer expectations and will have drastically changed the path to purchase. So, (AI) data gather tool is the predictive consumer expectations tool on every interaction, they have these brands.

4. Future (AI) can be impacted to influence consumer behaviors by its potential to free up time, enhance, quality, and enhance personalization. The industries include: Healthcare industry can apply (AI) to support diagnosis by detecting variations in patient data, early identification of potential pandemics, imaging diagnostics; automat industry can apply (AI) to autonomous fleets to ride sharing, semi-autonomous features, such as driver assist, engine monitoring and predictive, autonomous maintenance; financial service industry can apply (AI) to design the suitable personalized financial planning, fraud detection and anti-money laundering and automation of customer operation; transportation and logistics industry can apply (AI) to autonomous trucking and delivery, traffic control and reduced congestion and enhanced security; technology, media and telecommunications industry can apply (AI) to search media, and recommendation, customized content creation and personalized marketing and advertising to attract retailers to promote; retail and consumer industry can apply (AI) to design personalized production, anticipating customer demand, , inventory and delivery management; energy industry can apply (AI) to read and record smart metering , more efficient grid operation and storage and predictive maintenance; manufacturing industry can apply (AI) to enhance monitoring and auto-correction of processes, supply chain and production optimization and on-demand production.

Hence, future (AI) technology will impact consumer technology when any retailers apply it to assist its manufacturing processes or product sale or service provision processes to satisfy consumers' needs, it means that it can help any retailers to influence positive emotion to consumers in their whole sale or consumption or purchase processes

5. (AI) and machine learning technologies make it possible to capture, process, and inter data on a massive scale effectively , then any human being could ever do. For example, Criteo's creative technology " Kinetic design" can apply insights from 1.2 billion monthly impressions to select

and optimize individual branded advertisements components according to each shopper's preference and intent. This ensures more personalization and visually inspiring on brand ads. resulting in up to 12% more sales for (AI) technology advertiser clients.

Moreover, advertisers can now engage and inspire shoppers on a more personal level, rendering custom ads. it real-time for every impression. So, designer continues to learn from each design's success to make ads. more and more effective over time. Furthermore, brands are increasingly using paid search on retail sites to draw attention to their products on the crowded online shelf, e.g. Google shopping is a key growth area's more users are engaging with shopping ads. and across the globe. Google shopping has become essential to retailers' marketing strategies, but is a difficult channel to apply its tool to be promoted effectively . Thus, future (AI) and machine -learning technologies can dramatically improve digital commerce performance application to apply (AI) and machine learning to digital consumer. So, future (AI) technology can be applied to digital commerce aspect, it will fall into the categories of pattern recognition, classification, prediction and consumer behavior.

In conclusion, the benefits of using (AI) in digital commerce include: improved efficiency in discovering the relationships between datasets over traditional methods, which require complex modeling and coding, improved accuracy for clearly defined processes that involve a lot of manual processing, ability to deal with a large emotion of data with many attributes, for example: customer behavior data, multichannel and multi-device data , complex product data and fraud detection, more accurate analysis, such as customer segmentation sentiment, analysis and personalization frequent algorithum refreshes, such as several times a day, to capture the changes in customer and market behavior.

Finally, however, a lot of types predictive consumption behavior around (AI), in particulars that driven by vendors claiming their solutions are (AI) , ready and can deliver dramatic improvements over existing technologies. Application leaders for digital commerce can be misled into believing that (AI) can solve all their problems, which is not true for n in-depth discussion of the (AI) consumers and market behavioral predictive tool and machine -learning technologies bot. Thus, (AI) prediction consumer behavioral technology can give beneficial quantitative analysis for forecasting in business and market especially in consumer behavior and in the consumer decision-making process ( consumer choice model) more effectively and efficiently.


## Is Artificial Intelligent the most effective and accurate consumer behavioral tool?


Is (AI) the best and the most effective and accurate consumer behavioral prediction tool to compare other kinds of consumer behavioral prediction tools? Nowadays, retailing competitions are serious businessmen often find different kinds of methods to attempt to predict consumer changes. The consumer behavioral predictive methods can include as these below methods, instead of (AI) big data gathering tool.

Firstly, statistics is the popular mathematic method, it applies auto-regression, liner regression, structural equation modelling, logistic regression statistic techniques to be used to predict consumer behaviors. Secondly, it is classification method, it sis a support vector machine to assist businessmen to make consumer behavioral prediction, it also includes decision making tress diagram technique. Thirdly, it is rule mining method, it is algorithm, market base analytic etc. business marketing concept analytical tool, it also includes graph mining technique tool. Next, it is psychological prediction model tool, it is psychology prediction model too, it is a kind of psychological method to predict consumer behaviors. Finally, it is the most updated and potential artificial neural network (ANN) machine tool, it gathered big data, then it will carry on analyzing and applies psychological method to conclude the most accurate and reasonable solutions to give recommendation to businesses to predict when and how and why their consumer behaviors will change. So, it is one owned human mind's machine and owned psychological and analytical efforts to replace humans to make any judgement in order to make the most accurate predictive behavioral changes for consumers, instead of the traditional marketing concept and psychological and mathematic methods to predict consumer behavior, (AI) big data gathering tool will be another new tool.

What are the advantages of (AI) tool to be used to predict consumer behaviors as well as what are the different between it and other traditional consumer behavioral predictive tools? I shall explain as below:

Firstly, as above all case studies are explained to (AI) questionnaire design method benefit, I believe (AI) big data gathering tool can be applied to help human to analyze and design any the suitable valid questions to enquire any kinds of business consumers in order to gather the most meaning and useful opinions to conclude the most accurate consumer behavioral prediction for every questionnaire. So, future (AI)'s analytical effort and decision making effort most be exceed above human's judgement efforts. So, future (AI) can help human to design the most useful and meaning different kinds of valid questionnaire ( survey) questions as well as assist humans to analyze and make accurate decision making and conclusions to give opinions to help businessmen to predict when consumer behaviors will change and how their consumption behaviors will change to influence their businesses in order to help them to make any efficient and effective and accurate solutions to avoid consumer number to be decreased and the most important benefit is that it can give opinions to help businessmen to explain why ( what the factors ) cause their consumer behaviors change suddenly. It will be human's efforts can not achieve to exceed (AI)'s efforts in the future.

Secondly, (AI) can make artificial machine judgement and analytical effort, without human misleading or unfair or unreasonable judgement. So, it can make more fair and reasonable and accurate conclusion to give opinions to predict when, how and why consumer behaviors will change suddenly to the kind of business in customer model building process and evaluating the results of customer relationship management –related investment more accurate.

Furthermore, (AI) big data gathering tool will help businesses to improve the success rate of acquiring customers, increasing sales and establishing competitiveness. (AI) big data gathering tool can give opinions how to build customer loyalty to be positive emotion impact and it can find solutions to avoid every client's negative emotion causes to bring complaints behavior to the businessman's product or service. For example, Telecom industry and aggressive research has been conducted in this by applying various data mining techniques to avoid long distance phone call users' complaints. If gathered any long distance phone call users' past complaint data to record what are their general complaint issues. Then, (AI) tool will analyze all these past complaint issues to conclude and give opinions to let Telecom knows whether which aspects encounter challenge that Telecom needs to improve it's long distance phone call services or functions in order to satisfy Telecom's long distance phone call users' needs for long term. After Telecom attempted to improve its services and/ or functions from (AI) opinions and solution methods, when it fell it's long distance phone call users have positive emotions to satisfy its service performance and function performance. Then, it can prove (AI) tool's opinions and solutions are useful. The consequence is that their complain numbers will be decreased and they won't plan to choose another long distance phone call telephone service company to replace Telecom long distance phone call service more easily.

So, (AI) big data gathering tool can concentrate on finding focus on components of customer relationship management method and datasets more accurate and efficient and effective than human's data gathering and analytical effort. It implies (AI) big data gathering tool has unique more efficient and effective and accurate dataset gathering and analytical and judgement and decision making effort, it is human can not achieve.

Thirdly, (AI) big data gathering tool has much customer loyalty predictive effort. It's effort is more easily subsequently selected, reviewed and classified to compare human's gathering data effort in whole data gathering and analytical process.

In (AI) big data gathering process, (AI) can organize whole big data gathering process and technique more easily in short time. It will include these four steps. The first stage is that customer identification stage, customer identification also known as acquisition has to do with targeting the population , who are most likely to become customer segmentation. So, (AI) can help different kinds of businesses to gather their competitors' consumer purchase behavior data in short time, it is human can not achieve. The second stage is that customer attraction stage, after (AI) maker has been segmented for the business when it has ensured to gather the businessman's global competitors' consumers data. Then it analyze these all data to find solutions / methods to give the best opinions to the organizations how to achieve the direct effort and resources into attracting the target customer segments. The third stage is that customer retention, it can be defined as the activity that an organization undertakes in order to reduce customer defections. TO be successful, customer retention starts with the first contact on organization has with a customer and continues throughout the entire lifetime of a relationship involves loyalty programs, one to one marketing and complaints management. SO, (AI) can consist the business to find the best or the most reasonable , efficient , effective solutions or methods and it will conclude all these solutions to find the most reasonable and useful opinions to achieve to the aim to help the business to reduce customer complain numbers and help the business to build confident loyalty relationship between it and its clients. SO, (AI)'s analytical effort and decision making effort can be more accurate than human's analytical effort and decision making effort. IT can achieve it's consumer behavioral predictive aim more accurate and efficient and effective in the shortest time to compare human.

Fourthly, (AI) big data gathering tool can design more accurate dataset program for questionnaire (survey) to compare human's questionnaire ( survey ) effort. It means that (AI) can spend less time to research and make judgement what are the most reasonable and meaning questions for different kinds of businesses' needs. This includes data conduction a questionnaire, survey or interview of the individual or environment researched, public data repository: This includes commercially available public data; organizational data; this contains data collected from an organizational database, organizational information system. For example, their website log details etc. It also includes company transactional data, data purchased from a company.

For example, one vehicle sale company expects to research all global vehicle sale companies' past the different kinds of vehicle styles, design sale number data, the different kinds of vehicle style, design sale price data, every country's vehicle consumer number to the vehicle purchase number data to the vehicle company in short time. (AI) big data gathering tool can help the vehicle sale company to gather all any one for these global vehicle sale competitors' past data in the short time. It is human effort, who can not achieve this efficient, effective and accurate data gathering aim for this vehicle sale company. Even, when (AI) had gathered all global it's vehicle competitors' past sale data, (AI) can make more accurate analytical and judgement and decision making effort to design different kinds of questionnaire ( survey) questions to prepare to enquire it's different target segmentation vehicle potential clients in order to predict what are their needs to choose to buy any vehicles from the vehicle company. SO, (AI) tool can conclude more accurate conclusions and give the most reasonable and useful opinions to let the vehicle company to know in order to predict what are it's potential vehicle buyer's needs and manufacture the suitable vehicle styles or designs to raise their vehicle purchase desires.

Fifthly, (AI) tool is only one perfect tool for big data gathering in order to achieve accurate results and increased profit. What is (AI) big data gathering mean? The term " big data" gathering describes the accumulation and analytical of vast amounts of information, but big data is much more than a big amount of data. It is also the ability to extract meaning to sort through big volumes of numbers and find the hidden patterns, unexpected correlations and surprising connections that can be used in different industries like medical field, security and protection field or marketing that adopt " big data driven" decision making enjoy significantly greater productivity than those that do not. So, the benefits of (AI) is given to the company by using big data repaid complexity of implementation projects and hence project risks, when accelerating time to value. It is why that human's gathering effort can not replace ( A I ) data gathering effort.

All analysing above benefits to (AI) big data benefits to any organizations, it brief this question: How can (AI)apply big data gathering and analysing to predict when and how any why consumer behavior will change suddenly? The purchase decision making process is consumers reducing purchase choice behaviors.

Consumers are being considered pure rational beings ( consumer tried only to satisfy self-interest). Hence, due to future (AI) owns human's psychological , analytical , emotional predictive, purchasing decision making effort.

( A I ) will be assumed to sees one customer how who will make purchase decisions. So, after the (AI) gathered all data concerns the find of business's past customer segmentation purchase activities, e.g. age, sex,. Income level, the product's style sale number, the product price variable sale etc. different kinds complex data.

It can make more accurate psychological and analytical effort to predict when the business's consumer behaviors will change as behaviors will change as well as find what reasons their consumption behaviors will change and how trend of their consumer behaviors will change more accurate. For example, today there are a lot of industries that use big data: healthcare (treatment ) becoming personalized and patient centric and predictive analysis are used to prevent diseases for example Angelina Jolie under event a predictive double mastectomy after learning she had 87% rich to developing breast cancer, sports ( by using sensors data are collected from players during a game in order to improve their playing schemes), weather(more than 60 years of global weather analysis are used to predict the risk of future extreme events), logistics ( smart tucks and smart species, agriculture (monitoring weather and soil conditions for optimum point of harvesting).

Consequently, due to the evolving consumer demands, and the ever growing digitization, the world is digitally transforming which means the new technologies are needed to be used and driven significant business improvement. So, such as why (AI) tool will be our future main predictive tool to help businesses to predict when, how and why their potential customer behavioral will change. Big data is one of the our channels through digital transformation is made, together with cloud, mobile and networks. The challenges for digital transforming and therefore using A I
big data gathering tool as main technology are: digital proficiency, legacy systems, security and jobs becoming absolute.

In the future, big data can use data from text to picture , sounds, movies, music satellite coordinates or any other type of input or output data that type of input or output data that came from different influential aspect. It is cloud solutions, bring big data will be for predict insight driven by business strategy, new product strategies and new consumer relationship, predictive consumer behavioral strategy. Using the right data in the right business decision will mean smart decisions, new opportunities and utimately a big competitive advantage. Hence (AI) big data gathering tool is different is that (AI) can be one depth in-memory database function, it can make real-time data analytics that provide meaningful information in short time, it is also the visualization tool , such as SAP Lumira, allow this exploration and understanding of the data, and ultimately supports the decision making process. All above these features, which will be human's data gathering effort who won't exceed (AI) big data gathering effort. Hence, future (AI)big data gathering will be the best choice to assist businesses to predict consumer behaviors successfully.

Reference

Adrian, P. (2012). Introduction to marketing theory & practice, 3 rd edition, London: Oxford press.

Ajzen, I (1991). The theory of planned behavior. Organizational behavior and human decision processes, 50(2), 179-211. doi: 10.1016/0749.5978 (91) 90020-7.

Alba, Joseph W. and J. Wesley Hutchinson (1987). " Dimensions Of Consumer Expertise", Journal of consumer research, 13 March, 411-454.

Bailey, L., Mokhtarian, P.L. Little, A. (2008). The broader Connection Between Public Transportation, Energy Conservation And Greenhouse Gas Reduction, Report Prepared As Part Of TCRP Project J-11/Tasks Transit Cooperative Research Program, Transportation Research Board Submitted To American Public Transportation Association in http://www.apta.com/research/into/online/land_use.cfmi, accessed 17 April 2008.

Baucer, R,"Consumer Bhavior As Risk Taking , In Risk Taking And Information handling In Consumer Behavior", D. Coxceds Harvard University Press, Cambridge, Mass 1976.

Biederman, P. (2008). Travel and tourism, Pearson Prentice Hall, New Jersey.

Bogers, R. P., Brug, J. Van Assema, P., & Dagnetie, P.C. (2004) , Explaining fruit and vegetable consumption: The theory of planned behavior and misconception of personal intake level. Appetite, 42,157-166.

Bolton, Ruth N. (1998), " A Dynamic Model Of The Duration Of The Customer's Relationship With A Continuous Service Provider: The Role Of Satisfaction", Marketing Science, 17 (1), 45-65.

B.Shiv and A. Fedorikhin, " Heart And Min In Conflict: The Interplay Of affect And Cognition In Consumer Decision Making", J. Consumer Res., vol. 26, pp. 278-292, Dec. 1999.

Brown, K.W., Ryan, R.M. Reswell , J.D. (2007). Mindfulness: Theoretical Foundatins And Evidence For Its Salutary Effects. Psychological Inquiry, 18, 211-237.

Burke, R.R. : Behavioral effects of digital signage, J. Advertising Res. 49(2), 180-185 (2009).

Cant, M., Brink , A. & Brijall, S., Consumer behavior, Cape Town, South Africa: Juta, 2006.

Conner, M. & Abraham, C. (2001). Conscientiousness and the theory of planned behavior: Toward a more complete model of the antecedents of intention and behavior. Social psychology bulletin, 27, 1547-1561.

Cooper C. Mallon, K, Leadbetter S, Pollack L, Peipins ( 2005) , cancer internet search activity on a major search engine, United States 2001 to 2003, J Med Internet Res. 7(3): e36.

Cope, R. R. Cope and H. Davis (2008). Disney's virtual Queues: A strategic opportunity to co-brand services ? Journal of Business & economics research, vol. 6 no10, 13-20.

Cornelia, B.F. (1999) Rural development news, the North Central Regional Center For Rural Development vol. no 24 , IOWA.

Couper, M.P. J. Blair and T. Triplet ( 1999). A Comparison Of Mail And E-mail For a Survey Of Employees In USA Statistical Agencies. Journal Of Official Statistics, 15, 39-56.

David J. Nowak & Gordon M. Melsler (2016) " Air quality effects of urban trees and parks." National recreation and park association, USA.

Data monitor ( 2008). The proctor and gamble company. Retrieved Nov. 15 2009 from http://www.datamonitor.com/

De Hollander, A. E. M., J.M. Melse, Elebret & P. G.N. Kramers ( 1999), " An Aggregate public health indicator to represent the impact of multiple environmental exposures" Epidemiology: 606-617.

De Visser, R.O., & McDonnell, E.J. ( 2013). " Man points": Masculine capital and young men's health. Health psychology, 32( 1), 5-14. doi:10. 1037/a0029045.

Dunn, J & A Neumsister (2002). Knowledge management in the Information age. E. business review, Fall , 37-45. Jounral of service, spring 2011, vol. 4, no1, De Grovte (2009).

Dyer, D., F. Dalzell & R. Olegario ( 2004). Rising tide. Lessons learned from 165 years of brand building at Procter and Gamble. Boston, MA: Havard Business School Press.

Eysenbach G (2006) Infodemiology: Tracking flu- related searches on the web for syndromic surveillance. American Medical Informatics Associaion Annual Symposium Proceedings , Curran Associates, Red Hook, NY, pp. 244-248.

Ettredge M, Gerdes, J. Karuga , G (2005) Using web- based search data to predict macro-economic statistics. Commun ACM 48: 87-92.

Felce, D. and Perry, J. (1995). Quality of life: A contribution to its definition and measurement, vol. 16, no.1 pp: 51-74.

Feldman, Jack M. And John G. Lynch Jr. (1988), "Self-Generated Validity And Other Effects Of Measurement On Belife, Attitude, Intention And Behavior", Journal of applied psychology, 73(3),421-35.

Fiese, M, Hofmann, W., & Wanke, M (2009). The impulsive consumer. Predicting consumer behavior with implicit reaction time measurement. In M. Wanke (ed.) Social psychology of consumer behavior (pp.335-364). New York, NY: Psychology press.

Fitzsimons, Gavan, J. And Vicki G. Morwitz ( 1996), " The Effect Of Measuring Intent On Brand-Level
Purchase Behavior", Journal of consumer research, 23 (1), 1-11.

Hallerman , D. (2008) video Advertising Online: Spending And Pricing , New York. E-Marketer.

Harriet Griffey. (2010) The art of concentration, enhance focus, Reduce, stress and achieve move. Macmillan publishers ltd,Basinastoke and Oxford, London UK.

Helleman, D. (2008) Video Advertising Online: Spending And Pricing , New York, E-Marketer.

Hensen, C. (2003). Kreuzfahrtourismus.www.christoph- hensen.de/ Facharbeit.pdf.

Huang, H.I. (2012). An empirical analysis of the strategic Management of competitive advantage: a case study of higher technical and vocational education in Taiwan ( Doctoral dissertation,
Victoria University).

Jamieson, Linda F. And Frank M. Bass ( 1989), " Adjusting Stated Intention Measures To Predict Trial Purchase Of New Products: A Comparison Of Models And Methods," Journal of marketing research, 26 ( August), 336-45.


Korea Ministry Of Environment. Public Organizations spend 2.2 Trillon Korean Won To Purchase green Products in 2014; Ministry Of Environment: Sejoung, Korea, 2015.

Kremers, S.P. J., De Bruijn, G.J., droomers, M., Van Lenthe, F. J., & Brug, J. (2005). Environmental interventions for selected dietary behaviors in adults. In J. Brug & F. J. Van Lenthe ( eds.) , Environmental determinants and interventions for physical activity, nutrition and smoking: A review pp. 282-315. Rotterdam: Erasmus Medical Center.

Lee, D.; Kim, M. ; Lee, J. adoption of green electricity policies: Investigating the role of environmental attitudes via big data-driven search-queries. Energy policy 2016. 90, 187-201.
Lee, Terrence, " Tech in Asia-connecting Asia's startup system " Tech. in Asia- connecting Asia's startup ecosystem, N.p.,4 July 2016.

Los Angeles Country Department Of public Health (2016), Country Health Ranking Model, Retrieved From www.countryhealthrankgings.org/our-approach. USA.

Mayne, Lonnie. " Evolve of die in the age of the consumer". Entrepreneur, N.P. , 16 Apr. 2014. web of Oct. 2016.

McGregor, S.L. T., & Goldsmith, E.B. (1998). Expanding our understanding of quality of life, standard of living and well-being. Journal of family and consumer science, 90(2), 2-6, 22.

McMichael, A.J. M. Mckee, J. Shkolnikov and T. Valkanen ( 2004), " Morality trends and setbacks, global convergence or divergence?", Lancet 363, 1155-1159.

Melse, J.M. & A.E. M. De Hollander (2001). " Human Health And The Environment", background document for the OECD Environmental Outlook, OECD, Paris.

Moschis, George p. & Roy, L. Moore ( 1979), " Decision making among the young. A socialization perspective " Journal of consumer research , 6 ( September).

Mulligan, M. Banerjee, T & Thomas, N. (2008) ,European Paid Content And Activity Forecast, (2008 to 2013), Jupiter Research.

Peter, J., Ryan, M, M, " An Investigation Of Perceived Risk At The Brand Level, " Journal of marketing research, 13 May 1976, pp. 184-188.

Pieters, R., & Wedel, M. (2007). Goal Control Of Visual Attention To Advertising: The Yarbus Implication. Journal Of Consumer Research, 34, 224-233 ( August).

Parasuaman, and Leonard L. Berry (1985), " Problems And Strategies In Sevices Marketing", Journal of marketing, 49 ( Spring), 33-46.

Priesnitz, W. (2007) Counting Our Food Miles. Natural Life, 1 July.

R.C. Oliver, " When is consumer loyalty?" J.Marketing vol. 63, pp.33-44.1999.

Reggiani, A . (ed). 1998, accessibility, trade and locational behavior, Ashgate publishing ltd, England.

Rushe, D. (2013) " The 10 best paid CEO in America". The Guardian , 22 Oct, ( online). Available at: http://www.theguardian.com/business/2013/Oct22/best-paid-chief-executives-america (Accessed: 3 May 2014).

Spiekermann and Wegener (2007), update of selected potential accessibility indicators. Final report, urban and regional research ( S&W), RRG spatial planning and geoinformation. ESPON. Available online at http:// <www.espon.eu/mmp/online/website/ contentprojects/947/ 1297/file_2724/espon_accessibility_update-2006-fr_070207.pdf>, accessed on 1 July 2009.

Starbucks (2014) Our company available at http:// www. starbucks.com/about- us/company-information ( accessed: 3 May 2014).


Shostack, G. Lynn ( 1984), " Designing Services That Deliver", Harvard Business Review, 62 ( January-February), 133-9.

Shostack, G. Lynn (1985), " Planning The Service Encounter ,in the service encounter" , John A. Czepiel, Michael R. Solomon, and Carol F. Suprenant, eds. New York: Lexington Books, 243-54.

Shostack, G. Lynn (1987), " Service Positioning Through, Structural Change", Journal of marketing, 51 ( Janurary), 34-43.

Soloman, Michael R. (1985), "Packaging The Service Provider", Service Industries Journal , 5(1), 64-71.

Stevens, C.W. (1980), "K-MartStores Try New Look To Invite More Spending" The Wall Street Journal, Nov. 26, 29-35.

Sullivan, Nicholas P(2007). You can hear me now: How Micro loans and cell phones are connecting the world, San Francisco, CA: John Wilsey & Sans, 2007.


T. Ambler, A. Ioannides, And S. Rose, " Brand s On The Brain : Neuroimages Of Advertising ", Business Strategy rev., vol. 11, 3. pp. 17-30. 2000.

Westbrook, Robert A. ( 1980), " Intrapersonal affective influences on consumer satisfaction with products, " Journal of consumer research , 7 ( June) 49-54.

Wiig, k.(1993). Knowledge management foundations: Thinking About thinking. How people and organizations create, represent and use knowledge vol.1 , of knowledge management series schema press: Arlington, TX.

World Health Organization (2003). Diet, nutrition and the prevention of Chronic diseases report of a joint WHO/FAO. expert consultation. Geneva: World Health Organization.

Wysocki, B. (1979), " Sight, Smell, Sound: They're all arms in retailer's arsenal" The Wall Street Journal, Nov. 17, 1979. 1-35.

Yale Center For Environmental Law And Policy (2006). Environmental Performance Index. Data available on-line at http://epi.yale.edu